4/78

NO SOFT OPTIONS

ADMIRAL OF THE FLEET
SIR PETER HILL-NORTON

NO
SOFT
OPTIONS

*The Politico-Military
Realities of NATO*

WITH A FOREWORD BY HIS EXCELLENCY
DR J. M. A. H. LUNS
SECRETARY GENERAL OF NATO

LONDON
C. HURST & COMPANY

First published in the United Kingdom
by C. Hurst & Co. (Publishers) Ltd.,
1–2 Henrietta Street, London WC2E 8PS

© Sir Peter Hill-Norton, 1978

ISBN 0 905838 11 4

Printed in Great Britain

CONTENTS

FOREWORD

I am very pleased that Admiral of the Fleet Sir Peter Hill-Norton has taken the time to prepare this comprehensive volume about the North Atlantic Treaty Organisation. Sir Peter has had long experience with NATO, most importantly in his last post in which he rendered extraordinary service as Chairman of the NATO Military Committee, the highest military office in the Alliance. His experience lends to the book wisdom and insight which no outside observer could possibly bring to such a work.

Many of the realities which Sir Peter discusses are ones which have troubled the Alliance for many years. The book provides an excellent background for understanding these problems more clearly and I believe the reader will consequently appreciate more deeply the forces which have caused the Alliance to maintain its cohesion and credibility, despite the wide range of difficulties which it constantly faces. I hope the reader also derives a feeling for the concomitant fragility of the remarkable enterprise which NATO is and that this sentiment will be translated into more of a willingness to reinforce NATO's role in the defence of the West.

In May 1978 the Heads of State and Government of the fifteen member-nations of NATO meet in Washington to discuss the basic political and military state of the Alliance. Their deliberations will range over the entire spectrum of Alliance affairs, including East–West relations, as well as the military posture of NATO forces, and the conclusions they reach will have a far-reaching effect on the future of co-operation within the Alliance. I mention this meeting only because it clearly illustrates the importance which NATO member-nations attach to their mutual defence, as well as the time and effort which their leaders devote to Alliance problems. Sir Peter has performed a very useful task by identifying and explaining some of the most important NATO issues which face these statesmen and by suggesting possible new approaches to resolving some long-standing problems. In this sense he has made a contribution in terms of understanding the meaning of the 1978 Summit meeting, as well as the longer-term actions and decisions which come from it. Apart from being a welcome addition to the growing library of NATO literature, Sir Peter's book should be required reading simply on this point alone.

NATO Headquarters
Brussels
21 December 1977

JOSEPH M. A. H. LUNS
Secretary General

AUTHOR'S PREFACE

This is not even a small attempt at the definitive book about NATO. Nor is it a manual or a text book for use by students at military seats of learning or institutes of strategic studies. It is rather an attempt to describe why NATO was invented, how it came into being and has developed to the present day, and why its future strength and influence must be of overriding importance to all its members. In the process a good many facts have been rehearsed and some of the likely consequences of those facts have been suggested, by way of indicating the sort of problems which the Alliance has faced and will be called upon to face in the future, and the most promising ways of doing so.

Such a process is bound to include speculation upon options which certain courses of action have opened and closed, and the effect which decisions taken today will have, or could have, on both these and fresh options. Some of the received wisdom and some of the demonology, both in NATO Headquarters at Evere and in the capitals of member-countries, must find its place here as must some conceptions and misconceptions. I have thought it right to put some non-received wisdom alongside both Establishment views and those of their critics, in the search for a better-informed discussion of the actual instrument in which lies the best hopes of the Allies not only for their own security but for that of the world. In doing so, the opinions, unless otherwise expressly stated, are mine.

As Sir Andrew Huxley so shrewdly observed in his Presidential address to the British Association for the Advancement of Science in the summer of 1977, 'A sharp distinction must be drawn between questions of fact to be decided on evidence, and questions of the policy that should be adopted in the light of the facts.' I hope that all who care for the continued well-being of this great enterprise will approach all its affairs, as I have tried to do, in the same spirit. And not only today, for if I may adapt Sir Francis Drake, '. . . If it is given to thy servants to endeavour any great matter, grant them also to know that it is not the beginning, but the continuing of the same until it be thoroughly finished which yieldeth the true glory. . .' If ever there were a great endeavour of which those words were true, it is NATO.

Finally, I have done this work as a totally convinced NATO-man, who is proud to have held the highest military office in the Alliance as well as in my own country. For this reason the words 'we' and 'us' and 'our' should be taken throughout to mean NATO and its members, and not the United Kingdom or the British.

South Nutfield, Surrey   P.J.H.-N.
December 1977

CHAPTER I

INTRODUCTION: THE FIRST
TWENTY-FIVE YEARS

The North Atlantic Treaty was signed on 4 April 1949, and because it is at the heart of this book it has been reproduced in full, at Appendix B on page 160. The Treaty itself was, from the beginning, drawn strictly in the light of the Charter of the United Nations, and to save repetition Article 51 of that Charter is also reproduced in full, at Appendix A on page 159. It is appropriate as a point of departure for this examination of the Alliance today to look at where it had got to in 1974, after the first twenty-five years. During those years the early aims and perspectives, the hopes and fears and the consequent organisation had evolved into something very close to their present state. Happily the aims remained almost unchanged, the perspectives had been moulded and massaged by world events, the hopes had remained high and the fears had diminished. Predictably the necessarily somewhat *ad hoc* early organisation had been vastly extended, improved, refined and above all tested by the time of NATO's silver jubilee year.

Several definitive accounts of the origins and very early days of the Organisation have been published, of which perhaps the most complete and rewarding is that in Lord Ismay's book *The First Five Years*. There is a sufficiently full account for the beginner, covering a longer time-scale, in a publication by the NATO Information Service, revised every year or so and issued under the title *NATO Facts and Figures*. No attempt will be made here to re-cover this ground in the same sort of detail, but some account of this first quarter-century is necessary if the problems now facing the Alliance and their means of solution, and a forward projection of both, are to take their proper place in the general scheme of things. For only on a basis of the historical facts can it be assessed how well or otherwise the aims of the founding fathers have been achieved, the extent to which important factors affecting those aims have changed, the degree to which the evolution of the Organisation is meeting them and how fit the Organisation is to deal with the likely trends for the future. This is, and must be, a dynamic and not a static business.

The original twelve signatories of the Treaty may be said to have given birth to it out of a mixture of fear and necessity. There was fear because of the power vacuum created to the east and west of the Soviet Union by the defeat of Germany and Japan, and a clear perception that this vacuum was being filled already by the combined strength of the Red Army and world Communism. In the judgement of the new Allies there was a perceived danger that this combination was already embarked on an expansionist policy amounting in plain terms to the building of an empire, and thus creating a general threat to the hard-won peace and collective security throughout the Northern Hemisphere. It is relevant, and provides collateral if it is needed for this joint perception of danger, to look again at the telegram that Winston Churchill addressed to President Truman in May 1945. It read: 'What will be the position in a year or two when the British and American armies have melted away and the French have not yet been formed on any major scale and when Russia may choose to keep 200 or 300 divisions on active service?' And he added the famous sentence 'An iron curtain is drawn down upon their [the Russian] front. We do not know what is going on behind. . . .' To give added point to the fear which sired the necessity for collective military security, the combined total of all the Western armies had been reduced by 1946 from 5 million to less than 1 million men, while those of the Soviets had remained at their end-of-the-war strength of about 4 million. Few would question that this fear was then well founded. The necessity arose simply because it was totally clear that none of the Western powers could attempt to match military strength of this order alone.

As the Allies groped for collective security, a number of developments took place in the very early post-war days. Some, like the Truman doctrine enunciated in early 1947 ('It must be the policy of the United States of America to support free peoples who are resisting attempted subjugation by armed minorities or by outside pressure'), led immediately to very large appropriations for aid to Greece and Turkey, on which Soviet pressure had been brought hardest to bear. At about the same time General Marshall, then United States Secretary of State, initiated the idea of a programme for European recovery which led to the Marshall Plan. It is significant that Stalin refused all such aid, which was to have been made as freely available east of the Curtain as west of it, not only on behalf of the Soviet Union but on behalf of the satellite governments. Indeed he went so far as to set up the Cominform whose stated aim was to fight the Marshall Plan, which he described as an instrument of American imperialism. On the straightforward military security level, representatives of the United Kingdom, France and the Benelux countries met in Brussels early in 1948 to consider a treaty of mutual assistance. This quickly resulted in the Brussels Treaty, in which these countries pledged themselves to build up a common defence system, and significantly to strengthen their economic and cultural ties. For its military purposes the instrument of this Treaty was the Western Defence Committee, and this grew quickly into a formal organisation with Field Marshal Montgomery as Chairman and its headquarters at Fontainebleau—a going concern only six months after the Treaty was signed. This important European initiative was very rapidly followed up by the Americans when the following year the United States Administration decided to associate itself with the Brussels Treaty, and early in 1949, the Brussels signatories having invited Canada, the United States, Denmark, Italy, Iceland, Norway and Portugal to accede to the Brussels Treaty, the North Atlantic Treaty itself was signed in Washington. To complete the picture, it must be added that Greece and Turkey were invited to join the Alliance in 1951 and actually did so in 1952, to be followed by the Federal Republic of Germany, which officially became a member of NATO in May 1955.

It is important to record and remember that the North Atlantic Treaty thus signed is the framework for wide cooperation among its signatories, and has always been far more than a military alliance formed to prevent aggression or to repel it should it arise; indeed the Treaty expressly provides for continuing joint action in the political, economic and social fields. Thus the Organisation is dual in nature: it proclaims the importance of economic and social progress, while at the same time it reaffirms a security policy based on the inherent right of nations to collective self-defence. To jump ahead a little, it is of continuing importance and interest to note that although the founding fathers had in their wisdom created this dual approach from the beginning, first things rightly came first. And so during most of the first twenty-five years, with no dissent, the Allies agreed that only by the creation of military security could the other aims be successfully pursued. Hence, in practice, this aspect of their joint affairs took precedence over the others. By contrast, one observes today a perceptible change in this emphasis, since the successful achievement of tolerable military security has permitted wider-ranging and more detailed attention to be directed on political, economic and social affairs. The debate on which of these factors is now the chicken and which the egg, and indeed whether what was once the first has since become second, has been a source of endless discussion much enjoyed by the participants, and it is hoped that in the course of this narrative some conclusions about it may emerge.

Before discussing some of the events and circumstances which bore on the evolving machinery of NATO Government between the actual signing of the Treaty and the time when the dust had settled from the trauma of the French military withdrawal eighteen years later, it may be expedient to sketch first how the military and civil organisations began, grew and changed. This must involve some jumping back and forth in time, but it may reduce possible confusion over various Committees and Groups and their relations with one another.

Neither the civil nor the military evolution was particularly complicated, and with hindsight it is possible to say that circumstances would not have allowed the process to go much more smoothly or quickly than it did. To avoid misunderstanding, the whole civilian apparatus will here be called the 'political' side of the house, simply because it deals with policies and politics in the international sense, although only with the fall-out of national politics. In using this 'shorthand' it must be equally understood that many of the civilians serve military as well as political ends, and just as loyally. In this connection one of the great strengths of the International Staff is that its many essential officials and technicians are hired to be a-political, and to their great credit nearly always are.

Because it was to serve their aims that the military structure was created, the political side of the house, thus defined, will be dealt with first. We find that only a few short months after the Treaty was signed, it had been decided that supreme authority in the Alliance would be exercised by the Council composed of Foreign Ministers of the member-countries, and that it would meet once a year in regular session and, when necessary, additionally in extraordinary session. At the same time a Defence Committee composed of the Defence Ministers was also set up with a similar programme of meetings, and very soon afterwards a Financial and Economic Committee composed of Finance Ministers. This rather natural organisation proved too unwieldy and insufficiently responsive to deal with day-to-day events and routine business, and in 1950 the Council Deputies, sitting in London, were charged with the execution of the Council's directives and with coordinating the political (in the sense just defined) and military activities of the Alliance. In the following year, the Defence and the Financial and Economic Committees were stood down and the role of the Council Deputies, who thus began to look very much like the Permanent North Atlantic Council of today, was considerably enhanced. The imperatives of guiding the development and control of the Military side of the house led quite soon, as will be seen, to the re-activation of the Defence Committee, but the demise, as an institution, of the Finance Ministers' joint Alliance endeavours was permanent. This has had many disadvantages. As early as the Lisbon meeting of the Council in 1952, a rather more radical change to this basic structure was agreed and directed to the creation of a Council and Defence Planning Committee in genuinely permanent session. This has, broadly, remained unchanged to this day.

For this purpose Permanent Representatives at Ambassadorial level were nominated by each member, and formed (and still form) the North Atlantic Council and the Defence Planning

Committee (DPC), although since the withdrawal of France from the integrated military structure of NATO in 1966, and the announced intention of Greece to withdraw from it (which has not yet actually happened though many people think it has) in 1974, the DPC now sits at thirteen rather than fifteen.

The Secretary General is Chairman of the Council and the DPC at whatever level they meet. He is also Chairman of the Nuclear Defence Affairs Committee and the Nuclear Planning Group, the former having the same membership as the DPC less Iceland, and the latter being deliberately restricted to eight members of whom four are permanent and the others rotate. The Secretary General has a Deputy, also of Ambassadorial rank, who takes his place in all respects in his absence and who, with the Secretary General, directs the work of the International (political) staff.

To conclude this very brief and incomplete sketch, the business of the Council and the DPC is generated both in-house and in capitals, and is worked up and presented by the Executive Secretariat for discussion, amendment and eventual notation or approval. It should be borne in mind throughout all that follows that agreement has to be reached by common consent, with no provision for voting or majority decision, and that Council decisions once adopted become binding and can only be reversed by the Council itself. It should thus be clear that one of the most important functions of the Council, perhaps the most important, is the reconciliation of divergent views so as to arrive at the necessary unanimity. It should also be remembered that it follows from this *modus operandi* that one member, if intransigent for any reason, can frustrate all his colleagues indefinitely. Happily this is a rare occurrence, thanks to a great deal of very hard work and the admirable desire to reach agreement which illuminates the conduct of Alliance business. It is also a remarkable tribute to the skill, wisdom and determination of the succession of great men who have dignified the office of Secretary General.

Scampering as briskly over the essential landmarks in the development virtually from scratch of the Military Organisation, although the Brussels Treaty and its Western Defence Committee had given it both a lead and a flying start, we find that the concrete as it now exists was, on the whole, set with surprising and very creditable speed.

In 1949 the twelve founder-members had less than twenty divisions, twenty airfields and about 1,000 aircraft, and the maritime position was not much better. Nor was there any system of Allied command, control, communication or intelligence other than that which could be provided by as many disparate national arrangements as there were members.

The Military Committee, now the highest military authority in the Alliance and consisting of the Chiefs of Defence of all those nations which contribute forces to the integrated military structure (and thus not France or Iceland) with a Permanent Chairman, started its history two days before the Treaty was signed. In its very early days, with the approval of the Council (Foreign Ministers) and the newly created Defence Committee (Defence Ministers), the Military Committee consisted of one representative from each member-country, and it met for the first time in Washington in October 1949.

To assist (*sic*) the Committee in performing its tasks, an executive agency called the NATO Standing Group was created to function in continuous session. This Group comprised France, the United Kingdom and the United States as permanent members with each of the remaining Allies providing permanent representatives and technical and staff support to the Standing Group (not to the Military Committee). A year later these representatives were officially labelled the 'Military Representatives Committee' and, seven years after that, relabelled the 'Military Committee in Permanent Session'. This corresponded, effectively, with the formal designation of the North Atlantic Council in Permanent Session described earlier. The Standing Group, certainly for the first decade, did not in practice so much 'assist' the Military Committee as discharge its functions almost entirely. All the day-to-day business was done and all the day-to-day decisions were taken by this Group. Given the relative military and economic weakness of the remainder of the Allies, this was necessary and found acceptable by them, but as their recovery gathered momentum the activities of the Standing Group became, if not mildly resented, then certainly a cause for muttering. It was this which made necessary its development into the Military Committee and final establishment as such.

Before this came about and over the next few years, for very natural and sensible reasons, the Standing Group with its staff support was modified and strengthened by the inclusion and addition of staff planners to inject national guidance, and an International Planning Staff to pull it together composed of all the member-nations. Thus, in embryo, the present machine had by 1963 largely taken shape.

The final shove into the present organisation for Headquarters Military Management occurred when France withdrew from the integrated military structure in 1966, and the Headquarters of both the Council and the Military moved from both France and Washington to Brussels and were there, wisely, co-located. At this stage, at the direction of the Council, the Standing Group and its various higher, lower and equivalent appendages were stood down and the present organisation was established.

The North Atlantic Military Committee (whose development and evolution, powers and lack of powers, competence and scope, internal and external relations are worth a slim volume on their own) had actually opened for business in almost its present form under the chairmanship of General Heusinger two years earlier in 1964. Thus the French withdrawal was less a catalyst than the formal end of the beginning. The General and his successors were formally designated Chairman in both Chiefs of Staff (Defence) and Permanent Session. The Committee was then, and still is, served by an International Military Staff numbering today about 150 officers (450 all ranks) under a three-star Director. The Military Representatives, normally two- to four-star officers, are served by their own national staffs of varying sizes who must, and usually do, work on the whole cheerfully in very close co-operation with the internationals.

In parallel with all this the Command Structure developed. Under the three Major NATO Commanders, whom we shall meet again shortly, the geographical command boundaries were established and the subordinate commands designated. This Command Structure, too, is a subject on its own, out of place here, but it will be discussed in some detail in later chapters. It is worth noting the 'mission' (NATO-ese for responsibilities) of the Supreme Allied Commander, Europe (SACEUR) because the language is broadly applicable to the other international Commanders at all levels. It is, briefly, 'to ensure the security of Western Europe by unifying Allied Defence plans, strengthening Allied military forces in peacetime and planning for their most advantageous use in time of war'. The evident overlap between this formulation and the responsibilities of the Military Committee will also be more closely examined in a later chapter.

Turning from the evolution of the top of the management machine to more detailed matters, and to understand how and why the total situation facing the Allies changed during the first twenty-five years, one should remember that two major self-examinations and at least one major politico-military crisis have each forced an in-depth re-examination of the original concepts. The first was the very thorough look carried out by the 'Three Wise Men' in 1956, whose excellent work and compelling wisdom, officially known as the 'Report on Non-Military Co-operation in NATO', was adopted by the Council in 1956. Prior to this the Soviet challenge had been regarded as limited to Europe and essentially of a military nature, but by 1956 it was apparent that the Soviets were extending their influence all around the world, and that by then the challenge was also manifest in a variety of other forms, without any diminution of the military threat itself. By adopting the report of the Three Wise Men, the Council gave a new dimension to their political span of control, with the result that today it covers practically every subject of common interest and has the prime object of developing a joint posture in the formative stages of the evolution of national policies. Twelve years later the Council approved the Report on 'Future Tasks of the Alliance', more generally known as the Harmel Report. Although dedicated from the outset, both individually and collectively, to the relaxation of tension in Europe, the fifteen member-Governments, in adopting this Report, expressly undertook to pursue a positive policy of seeking realistic solutions to all issues which could further East–West détente.

This policy is still very much at the heart of NATO's endeavours, although its detractors seek to persuade us otherwise, and in spite of being expressly included in the simplest definition of NATO strategy, the fact that it is a cornerstone of NATO policy is too often forgotten.

The orderly progress on both sides of the house to a recognisable Management System which has just been described was not only interrupted, but given added urgency, by the Communist attack on South Korea in 1950. This led the North Atlantic Council to consider positively how to defend the NATO area against possible aggression similar in style to that used in Korea, and it was unanimously agreed that a forward strategy must be adopted for Europe. In other words, any aggression should be resisted as far to the east as possible, even though it was recognised that such a strategy would demand forces far exceeding those available to NATO at the time. Thus it was that the Defence Committee was requested by the Council to plan for the creation of an Integrated Force under centralised command which would be adequate to deter aggression. So was born what remains to this day the central feature of Allied military security. This was, of course, five years before the Federal Republic of Germany joined the Alliance, and very difficult problems obviously arose for the Defence Committee and the Standing Group in attempting to carry out their mandate. In spite of these problems, and thanks to their determination and a jointly felt sense of urgency, the first Supreme (Allied) Commander Europe (SACEUR) was appointed in 1950 in the person of the greatly respected and universally popular General Eisenhower, and this coincided happily in time with the appointment of the first Secretary General, the equally respected and popular General Lord Ismay. Two years later, at the Lisbon meeting of the Council, the other two major NATO commands were established as Allied Command Atlantic and Allied Command Channel.

It must be a source of profound satisfaction to those who met at this historic Council in Lisbon twenty-five years ago to note that the basic structure and organisation which their collective wisdom and courage devised have so successfully stood the test of time and change.

The very dramatic withdrawal of the French armed forces from the integrated military structure of the Alliance had, fairly obviously, a number of important consequences for NATO and indeed for France. The political decision by France to make this withdrawal included a request that all international headquarters, Allied units and installations not under the direct control of the French Government should be removed from French territory. The remaining Allies swung briskly into action at all levels, and a group under the chairmanship of M. André de Staercke, the Belgian Permanent Representative, worked out and carried through the negotiations with France on behalf of the fourteen. Thanks to the determination, ability, wisdom and vast experience of M. de Staercke, these negotiations were successfully concluded within a year, and as a result of their rapid and successful progress it was possible for the Council in Ministerial session to take several important consequential decisions only a few months after the event. These included, as has already been mentioned, the co-location of the Military Committee with the Council at Evere and the transfer of SACEUR's Headquarters to Mons about 60 kilometres away.* Apart from the urgent and pressing problems of re-location and reorganisation, of which the most stubborn were thus quickly and happily resolved, the French withdrawal created many other problems some of which will be referred to in a later chapter. But paradoxically the event, which of course was headlined as a crisis, undoubtedly concentrated the minds of both military leaders and their political partners in a way which led very quickly to the much smoother and more effective organisation upon which NATO today still essentially relies.

---

* It is agreeable to note in passing that ten years later, when André de Staercke had been the Belgian Permanent Representative for twenty-five years, Her Majesty Queen Elizabeth II was pleased to confer on him the quite unusual distinction in such circumstances of a Knight Grand Cross of the Order of St. Michael and St. George, and the author, who was present when this was announced, may be allowed to add that this was emotionally and happily received not only by this great man but by every one of his colleagues, the entire Military Committee and every man and woman in the Headquarters in Brussels.

Thus by 1967 the basic Organisation had developed; a Nuclear Defence Affairs Committee and its Nuclear Planning Group had been formed; the First Five Years Force Plan—then as now the heart of the work of the Defence Planning Committee and almost the only real discipline exerted from Brussels—had been developed; and the first comprehensive review of NATO strategy since 1956 had been completed. There were of course other milestones. The original military strategy of a trip-wire and massive retaliation to which the Alliance was driven by the gross imbalance of conventional power was, with predictable difficulty, finally articulated in a Military Committee document approved by the Council which, until it was superseded, amounted to Holy Writ.

The rapid development by the Soviet Union of strategic nuclear weapons soon cast doubt on the continuing validity of this as a sensible, or indeed plausible, instrument of deterrence. It was increasingly often asked—and reasonably enough once the ability was demonstrably there—whether the Americans were actually ready to have Chicago 'taken out' in order to deter (by taking out, for example, Leningrad) a two-division assault on Finnmark. Happily this potentially divisive strain on the cohesion of the Alliance was never put to the test. The Allies wisely concluded, even before the two super-powers had reached approximate parity in strategic nuclear weapons, that the Holy Writ needed to be brought up to date—in close analogy, without disrespect, to the writing of a New Testament.

The task of re-writing such immensely revered and universally obeyed received wisdom put little strain on the wits or imagination of the military and political strategic planners because it was, and still is, fairly obvious what had to be done. The strain on the hearts minds and nerves, the stamina and determination, and the ingenuity and flexibility of the drafters was, by contrast, extreme. But it got done, by patience and wisdom and the imperatives of the actual situation. And so in 1967 the Military Committee laid their second egg (in this nest), enshrining the doctrine of 'deterrence, forward defence and flexible response, with détente' which is unchanged (and highly unlikely to be changed) to this day. This too was quickly approved by the Council, and moulds all NATO thinking and planning in a realistic and practical way. It does not pretend to make it easy, but it does make the objectives very clear.

This exercise is an excellent, perhaps the best, demonstration of the fact that NATO is dynamic and not static. Its tablets, although written and clearly written and having the magisterial authority of stone, are in practice found to be of a softer material (but not in any other respect) so that changing circumstances can, and have been, met with changed policies.

Détente was still to the forefront when the Council, meeting in Iceland in 1968, took the first and vital step along the road to mutual and balanced force reductions (MBFR) in what has become known as 'The Reykjavik Signal'. But the hopes of stabilisation and détente which this had raised, and not only in NATO, were sharply set back almost at once by the rape of Czechoslovakia. Allied discussion of this crisis culminated in the unanimous declaration of member-Governments in the Council that the Soviet military intervention was a clear violation of the UN Charter and of international law, and this was followed by a warning to the Soviet Union that any further such intervention, directly or indirectly affecting the situation in Europe or in the Mediterranean, would create an international crisis with grave consequences. Subsequent to this a number of measures calculated to improve the overall NATO defence posture were quickly put in hand, as for example the co-ordination of maritime air reconnaissance operations in the Mediterranean, the concept of an Allied naval on-call force in the same sea, and a special command activated in Naples to control them. All this, contrary to what has so frequently been asserted by NATO's detractors, indicates by any standards a positive and vigorous reaction to a serious challenge.

There were perhaps only a few subsequent developments which merit a mention in this very short and deliberately over-simplified account of the first twenty-five years. The United States and the Soviet Union began their bilateral Strategic Arms Limitation Talks (SALT) in 1969, and at about the same time a highly important initiative began within NATO. The so-called 'A.D. 70' (Allied Defence in the 1970s) study was put in hand with a view, for the first time, to taking a look at the military structure for the ten years ahead. In parallel with this joint appraisal, but worked out separately, the European Defence Improvement Programme (EDIP) was undertaken by the European member-states so as to provide a very large sum indeed, independent of the North American contribution, for both political and military improvements. A year later preparations began for the start of the Conference on Security and Co-operation in Europe (CSCE), and finally the Yom Kippur war broke out in October 1973. This grave event, although outside the NATO area, provided clear evidence that the danger of a sudden aggression was still a very real one and that it was correspondingly important to keep the means of dealing with it up to date. It also meant, regrettably, that the process of détente now demanded a guarded approach, its present limits having become suddenly apparent although, perhaps on the credit side to balance this disappointment, the crisis certainly vindicated the wisdom of the concept repeatedly proclaimed by the West that détente and security are indivisible. And so the twenty-fifth anniversary of the signing of the Treaty arrived on 4 April 1974 and was celebrated in a somewhat muted way at NATO Headquarters and the Headquarters of the Supreme Allied Commanders.

It is appropriate to conclude this brisk *tour d'horizon* on NATO's birth, youth and early maturity with reference to the Ottawa Declaration, because it sums up neatly how far the Organisation had progressed by 1974, and unambiguously re-states its aims. As a conscious act of policy it was, as part of the events marking the twenty-fifth anniversary, thought both desirable and necessary publicly to re-affirm both the spirit and objectives with which the Alliance determined to face the future. After careful preparation, and a happy absence of contention, the Declaration (reproduced in full at Appendix C on page 164) was adopted by the North Atlantic Council in Foreign Ministers session at Ottawa on 19 June 1974 and signed in Heads of State and Government session in Brussels a week later. This historic document deserves careful study by well-wishers and critics alike. So clear are the fourteen articles that comment on them in this text would be superfluous.

This brief account should serve to make clear what NATO is and what it is not. It is, as the Treaty expressly sets out, an organisation of like-minded states joined together to preserve peace and international security and to promote stability and well-being in the North Atlantic area, whose members undertake to eliminate incompatibility in their economic policies and to encourage economic co-operation among themselves. It is a treaty of alliance, within the framework of the United Nations Charter, for the defence of a way of life, not only by military means but also through co-operation in political, economic, social and cultural fields. Although many people wish and some even believe otherwise, it is not an organisation, and specifically not a supra-national organisation, which offers to police the world or to settle quarrels among its members. It is without doubt the most, and perhaps the only, effective foundation for the security of each of the Allies. It therefore follows that continuing support for this great enterprise must be an imperative of all our policies until a braver new world dawns.

CHAPTER II

THE THREAT

People continually ask whether there is a threat to NATO or to its individual member-states. Others go further and assert that there is no threat. I find this strange, and this chapter seeks to explain why. It is, just possibly, necessary to assert that the word 'threat' itself in this context means—let there be no possible misunderstanding about it—a threat to the very way of life which the Allies have chosen. Within this concept the threat may include loss of sovereignty, loss of territory or loss of money on a national scale, and it may be posed by military power or action as well as by direct political pressure or blackmail or, more subtly, by economic measures. Fortunately it is not necessary to examine these manifold elements of it in order to discuss the threat itself.

It must at once be said that it is impossible to prove that there is such a threat, although reasonable men can make acceptable deductions from observed facts and this also will be attempted shortly, and it is, of course, equally impossible to prove that there is not a threat at all; but it is certainly less easy, and indeed could be judged impossible, acceptably to deduce that this is so from the same observed facts. At all events, the founding fathers of the Alliance certainly thought there was one as early as 1947; so indeed did the Governments of the United Kingdom and of all the Allies, and whichever political parties have been in power ever since have continued to think the same way, and to express that thought publicly. In the improbable event that the doubters and the 'no-threat' men dispute this, it is necessary only to refer to the preamble to the Treaty which says: 'It is a treaty of alliance within the framework of the United Nations Charter for the defence of a way of life not only by military means but also . . .', and to Article 2 which defines the aims to be followed by member-countries in their international relations, and indicates particularly how these aims should be fulfilled. This, so the Treaty holds, is inspired by Article 1 of the United Nations Charter which defines, among the aims of the United Nations, the preservation of peace and the development of friendly relations among nations. Articles 3 and 4 of the North Atlantic Treaty also refer expressly to the ways and means of maintaining and increasing the individual and collective capacity of members to resist armed attack and the obligations to do so incumbent on member-countries. Perhaps the most important provision of the Treaty in any context is that in Article 5 which states: 'An armed attack against one or more members in Europe or North America shall be considered an attack against them all.' It can hardly be supposed that those who used formal language of this nature in a solemn and binding Treaty could have perceived no threat.

This perception was based, of course, on the actual and observed policies of expansion, and indeed conquest, on the Soviet side of Churchill's 'curtain' and the simultaneous reduction and contraction of military power and the shedding of Empire on the other. One merely has to think of the pressures which effectively drove Bulgaria, Romania, East Germany, Poland, Hungary and Czechoslovakia to fall within the sphere of Soviet domination to identify the expansion and aggression which was happening. And it is sobering to remember that this involved an area of about 390,000 square miles and a population of over 90,000,000 non-Russian inhabitants. Nor did this relentless pursuit of domination occur only in Europe (where it was successful). It was happening also in Northern Iran, Manchuria, North Korea, Indo-China, Malaya, Borneo and the Philippines (in most of which it was not successful), so it can hardly be deemed that the founding fathers were un- reasonable in deducing that a threat existed. If this needed any confirmation, it was at once given by the Soviets themselves, who saw fit publicly to denounce the North Atlantic Treaty, shortly before it was signed, as a hostile act liable and likely to increase tension.

Possibly even if driven by these undeniable facts to accept that there was a threat immediately after the Second World

War, the 'no-threat' men (who on the whole do not like facts) might shift their ground and deny that one still exists today. But the same basic consideration must surely apply here, as it must in any other respectable process of forming a judgement, in the way that Sir Andrew Huxley demanded of examining the facts whether they are convenient or not, and making reasonable deductions from them. These facts will be rehearsed in detail in Chapters IV and V, where the military balance today and its forward projection are discussed in detail, and the same reasonable deductions, *mutatis mutandis*, as those which persuaded the founding fathers thirty years ago that they were threatened, will be seen still to apply. The Alliance is formally pledged to seek the orderly resolution of international disagreements; it is equally pledged to, and indeed could be held to have initiated, the process of détente, and there is no lack of willingness in the governance of the Alliance to seek explanations for facts which might lead to the reasonable deduction that no threat to its members exists today. But it cannot be done.

Whether the doubters and 'no-threat' men accept this (and they must do so in their heads if not in their hearts), and whether deductions are held to be reasonable or unreasonable, there is a simpler, although not simplistic, approach to the formation of policy, which is to accept the universally adopted definition of a threat as being a compound of capability and intention. Let us examine this classical definition as it applies to the circumstances which actually confront us. It is now widely known and accepted that capability can today be measured with very great precision by a host of modern means, some very sophisticated and others as simple as the naked eye. We know (and we must suppose that as much is known about NATO) precisely how many divisions are in the Warsaw Pact order of battle. Leaving aside for this rather narrow purpose the nuclear arms, we know how many pieces of artillery, armoured fighting vehicles, elements of bridging equipment and men are deployed and how many of each are in reserve. We know how many different types of warship on and under the sea there are, and with what weapons systems they are equipped. We know how many squadrons of aircraft are deployed by type and role and what kit they carry, and the same is true across the whole spectrum of offensive and defensive military arms. And to continue the catalogue we know the rates of production of all these elements, and they are frightening.

We do not know the intentions of the Soviet leadership, and it is in the highest degree unlikely that we ever shall. It is at least fair comment that in the climate of the late 1970s, with perfectly reasonable demands for increased expenditure on social services, schools, hospitals, roads, welfare, housing and wages, and in the climate of endless talk about détente, speculation on intentions is almost certain in the Western democracies to be on the over-optimistic side. And it has been historically demonstrated over centuries that such democracies have always found it difficult to devote more than the rock-bottom insurance premium to defence after many years of peace. In this matter NATO is to some extent a prisoner of its own brilliant success: not a shot has been fired, not a man killed, nor a square millimetre of ground lost to an external aggression in the thirty years since the Treaty was signed. So it is attractive to assert that the threat has gone away. Yet it is a soft option and, like all soft options, almost certain to lead to faulty assessments and unwise decisions.

But what is sure, and cannot be denied, is that capability in the military sense takes certainly not less than seven and probably ten years, to create. Countless examples lie to hand— of which perhaps the most telling is that with absolutely un-limited resources of men and material and with relentless determination and drive, it took that great man Admiral Gorschkov fifteen years to create the global all-purpose Soviet Navy whose flag (as he says) now flies on every ocean of the world. But, by contrast, intentions—even in the highly unlikely event that they were known in the first place—can change overnight. And what is equally certain is that the intentions of the Communist leaders are almost certain to change as those who exercise that power change, either by due political process or more certainly through age.

So to the 'no-threat' men it can be said, one hopes without fear of contradiction, that the facts are against them. And to everybody else it can be said that in the light of the absolute differences between capability and intentions it would be the height of folly to base one's own policy on intangibles when precisely measurable certainty about capability lies to hand.

It is comforting that the fifteen Governments which make up our great Alliance have taken and still take this view. Why else, despite immense social and political pressures, have they devoted, and do they still devote very large resources to individual and collective defence? The answer is 'Not for fun.' More precise, and more factual, illustrations of what resources they do devote and whether these are enough will be given in later chapters—which may not prove that there is a threat, but which will quite certainly prove that the fifteen Allied Governments think that there is.

CHAPTER III

DETERRENCE

It cannot be too loudly stated or too often repeated that Deterrence is the name of the NATO game. The whole NATO enterprise is about deterrence and everything within the Alliance in terms of men, weapons, command and control, communications and the political direction and the economic co-operation are there simply and solely to create and sustain this one overriding element. As every Article of the Treaty makes clear, NATO is by definition a collective defensive alliance—this was discussed in some detail in the first chapter— and while it has long been said that 'attack is the best method of defence', in the circumstances of NATO it is even better to deter.

What then is deterrence? This is a highly subjective matter about which no certainty can exist. It cannot be measured or touched, it cannot be seen or heard, but it can certainly be felt. In the simplest terms it is successfully achieved when those who wish to deter are not attacked. Thus in a sense it is a negative concept, but it is one with highly positive results.

Before discussing this elusive notion further it is as well to say flatly what it is not, because a great deal of time and nervous energy, as well as paper, words and pictures, have been spent on misinformed discussion of what deterrence is, when in fact such discussion has all too frequently generated great heat about what it is not. It is above all not war fighting. Certainly the perceived ability to fight is an essential ingredient of it, and the perceived ability to fight is precisely what is meant in that element of NATO strategy described as flexible response (which means quite simply the ability to fight at any level). There are of course many other essential ingredients but they are the brush strokes on the larger canvas.

There are indeed only a few major elements in deterrence.

The most evident is the military capability to match aggression at all levels from bullying or harassment, from minor incursions or probes or adventures, to limited war by land sea or air up to what has lately been called the 'standing-start blitz', and finally to general war and a strategic nuclear exchange. And this is measurable. It is not, however, sufficient simply to create a military capability which is adequate to produce this element of deterrence unless this capability is backed by the political will first to continue to allocate sufficient resources to preserve it at the requisite level, and secondly to fight—and to be known to be ready to fight—should deterrence fail. This cannot be measured.

It is agreed by the signatories of the North Atlantic Treaty, with total clarity in Article 5, that an attack on one (but only in Europe or North America) will be regarded as an attack on all. And to discharge this solemn joint responsibility the two elements of deterrence just mentioned are those which are vital. They imply the will and the means to create in all three elements, and in time and space, the means and method for a flexible response. The search is for credibility, and this in the mind of any potential aggressor is of first-rate importance. However, close to it must equally lie credibility in the minds of all the partners in this great Alliance.

For many years even quite well-informed people spoke as if deterrence meant strategic deterrence, and nuclear strategic deterrence at that. This was no doubt because, in the early years, NATO's strategy—and thus deterrence—was indeed based upon a trip-wire adequate to identify aggression but not intended to deter *per se*, and upon massive nuclear retaliation which was intended to deter all forms of aggression. Even before the time when approximate parity in strategic nuclear weapons was reached, this notion was beginning to look rather unreal and, as has been described in Chapter I, the strategy was formally changed. The essential point is that NATO's deterrence has not been about only nuclear deterrence for many years, and it is thus worth reflecting for a moment on the notion of deterrence as such in terms of the means of achieving it.

An unarmed policeman on the beat is a deterrent to a large number of crimes. In military terms, perhaps the lowest forms of deterrent are, say, an electric fence, a guard dog and a searchlight. Some way further up this very long ladder of deterrence comes the single soldier with a modern musket. Multiply him up and automate his weapon, put them all in an APC, and a platoon of mechanised infantry will safely deter much more serious crimes than the unarmed policeman. And so on to the armoured division with air support, sophisticated communications and intelligence and we are getting into the big league of deterrence. Without extending this line of thought, it may be said that in the general debate too little attention has been paid to what is likely to deter what, and in consequence there exists no agreed yardstick by which to measure what is the best value for money in this class of work. For example, what is elegant and simple and cheap and will do the job? On the NATO scale not much—more's the pity—but more than most pundits of the high-technology, big-battalion schools are ready to concede.

There is a further and equally unquantifiable feature of this elusive notion which might be loosely described as the 'ten-feet high' syndrome. It is, perhaps, a natural law that in many fields of human endeavour the prudent operator tends to think that his adversary or competitor is cleverer or taller or richer or stronger than he is. There are, of course, less wise men who in similar terms underrate the opposition. In the search for deterrence the balance will best be struck by those who remember first that the opposition is probably erring on the prudent side; and secondly that it is more than likely that you are both about the same size unless reliable observation makes it certain that this is not so.

The effect of these fancies on actual deterrence is probably self-cancelling to the extent that our reasonable man, particularly if such is his job, can be reasonably sure what will *not* do if he is dealing with a reasonable opposition. He can also make an informed guess ('assessment' is the more fashionable word but in the circumstances it is pretentious) as to what *will* do, certainly in military terms. It is, sadly, much easier to spell this out in political terms but also much easier to get it wrong, even badly wrong, and this is highly dangerous. This is not because the military are brighter or have better crystal balls but simply because they are dealing with things that can be seen and measured, rather than ideas which can not. This is a not entirely dissimilar line of thought to that about capability and intention discussed in the last chapter.

A good example of the different perceptions of deterrence in the political and military fields was the statement by Lord Home of the Hirsel, in a lecture to the Royal United Services Institution in London in October 1977, that '. . . the Allies have now reduced expenditure on conventional arms to a point where we are back to the policy of the "trip-wire", that in response to any attack on Germany by the Soviet Union armies [*sic*] the tactical nuclear weapon would have to be used at once.' Such words from a wise and experienced former British Prime Minister and Foreign Secretary, who has also been a supporter of the Alliance and its defence throughout its life, must carry great weight, but I must regretfully disagree with him. Although as Chairman of the Military Committee I was frequently obliged to sound sombre warnings of the immense dangers of reductions in our conventional capabilities, I do not believe that NATO has by any means reached such desperate straits. Nor do the two Supreme Commanders. But if Lord Home were right, then our whole deterrent posture would be suspect and this would amount to a gravely de-stabilising factor not only in East–West relations but within the Alliance itself.

Although deterrence is an abstract notion, and thus does not lend itself readily to factual argument, there are, as has just been said, some judgements about what will do and what will not do on which it is worth briefly reflecting. It has been said, and hardly any informed observer would disagree, that a trip-wire and massive nuclear retaliation will not do. Both super-powers are now capable of an invulnerable strategic nuclear second-strike which would totally destroy the capacity of the other to continue a war by any means, and probably destroy organised society as well. The French and the British strategic nuclear deterrents are, on a smaller scale, capable of inflicting what has been called 'unacceptable' damage on the Soviet Union. In this situation it simply is not to be believed that deterrence can any longer be achieved by the original NATO strategy. Certainly the strategic nuclear arsenal must remain the ultimate sanction if all other means of safeguarding our vital interests were to be exhausted, but on the way up to that topmost rung of the escalation ladder (which it is in the interests of the whole world never to reach) there must be credibility on each of the lower rungs, which we call the flexible response. There are very strong arguments, which will be dealt with at some length in the next chapter but one, for not resting or relying on theatre nuclear weapons, which is the next rung down, although at this level too deterrence demands the possession and perception of adequate strength. But the whole of deterrence could certainly not be achieved by these weapons alone.

In the catalogue of things which would not do must also be recorded any gross imbalance between the sea, land and air forces of which we dispose, or even an imbalance within any one of those elements between any specialised arm or capability. Land forces must have their armour, their artillery and their infantry, and all the range of equipment which enables these arms to operate in mutual support as well as in their specialised role. No army lacking any one of these elements and all the others which have not been mentioned could deter an attack. In precisely the same way maritime forces must be capable of anti-submarine, anti-surface and amphibious operations, all to be conducted securely in a hostile air environment; and air forces must be equipped and trained for air defence, interdiction (counter-air operations by attack on enemy bases or lines of communication), ground-support, reconnaissance, intelligence gathering and radar-jamming missions. The absence of any of these, at sea or in the air, would leave a perceived hole in our defences—the legendary chink in our armour—which would not only seriously diminish the deterrent effect of the re-mainder but, much more dangerously, would almost invite a would-be aggressor to exploit the weakness. So another thing which will plainly not do is to fail to arm ourselves throughout the whole spectrum of modern war. This points most of the way to forming a view—it can never be more—of what will do.

In the end, most of the above considerations concern the functions of quality, and it must be said at once that quality and quantity are the two measurable terms in the military equation. They are to some extent, but only to some extent, interdependent in the sense that one really advanced anti-tank weapon can be worth two or three of any earlier generation or, in another sense, can greatly redress a quantitative advantage in tanks. The same type of arithmetic can be applied to the whole inventory of weapons systems and this has to be given due weight when forming the view of whether our quantity plus quality add up to enough to deter whatever is the sum of the terms on the other side of the equation. It must be repeated here, because it is the essence of deterrence, that they do not have to be equal to succeed in this aim. This, of course, instantly brings up the important factor that even a very substantial qualitative advantage can never wholly compensate for a gross disadvantage in quantity. Striking an accurate balance between the two is another exercise in judgement of what will do and what will not do, and here too it is always easier to say what will not do. Some more detailed discussion about the conventional balance will be found in the next chapter, but for the purpose of trying to harden the argument about the nature of deterrence, it can at once be said that there is a critical level of power, made up of quantity and quality, at which deterrence can be achieved, and if we fall below that level, it will not. Here, then, is the rub. What, everyone wants to know, is that level? The question has attracted more discussion than any other single aspect of NATO's military life, and will continue to do so. It has been sharpened and intensified by the adverse trend in the balance of conventional forces, to our disadvantage, which has been so sombre a feature of the last few years. The question, as this chapter has set out to make clear, cannot be answered with any precision. If, in a European war, one side has 10,000 tanks, then it plainly will not be deterred from an armoured thrust if the other side has only 1,000, although it certainly would (other things being more or less equal) if it had 7,000. What about 6,000, 5,000, or 4,000? Somewhere at the lower end of this scale lies the answer, influenced, as has been explained, by the relative qualities and the impact of associated arms. It is this sort of exercise which must be applied across the NATO board before the value judgement can be made. But it remains, and always will, a very inexact science if it is a science at all.

There are some further elements of deterrence, apart from these matters of numbers and quality, which must be mentioned, even though they are still less capable of being quantified. The quality of the men engaged has always been critical to the winning and losing of battles, not only through their sheer competence as a result of education and training but also through their morale. This quality is enhanced or degraded to a highly significant extent by their leadership, and some more is said about this too in the next chapter. Strategic and tactical planning and the execution of those plans depends not only on the quality of the Commanders but on the means with which they are provided to exercise their command. In all this group of comparisons NATO is well placed and known to be well placed. To that extent, the deterrent value of the quantity and quality of their order of battle is enhanced. About this too no one can say by precisely how much.

These, then, are some of the more particular elements (though still not facts) which must be taken into account when assessing whether or not our military effort is adequate to deter. Careful study of each of them will also quickly reveal weaknesses, and provides the framework within which a judgement may be formed about whether NATO's Force Plans meet the requirements on which our whole policy must rest. All this adds up to a very simple statement—that deterrence is all about creating a fearful doubt in the mind of a potential aggressor that any likely gain is simply not worth the inevitable risks. This is the name of the NATO game.

CHAPTER IV

THE CONVENTIONAL BALANCE

Any attempt to assess precisely the balance of conventional (in this context non-nuclear) military power between NATO and the Warsaw Pact will inevitably be incomplete and is bound to be hedged about with reservations, because a true balance, as this chapter will attempt to show, can not be quantified, although certain elements of it can be. It would be agreeable if all the elements in the scales could be presented in the form of a simple balance-sheet with NATO on one side and the Warsaw Pact on the other, but it would be quite misleading. Moreover this sort of numerical comparison already exists in many publications of which probably the best, and the most readily available, is *The Military Balance*, published annually in London by the International Institute for Strategic Studies. Regrettably all these are somewhat daunting (and bound to be so) for the general public and, worse, the bald statistics have gloomy implications for them and thus can also tend to mislead. In spite of these difficulties it is crucial to an understanding of what NATO is doing, and how and why it is doing it, to have a clear and objective view of this conventional balance, because it is fundamental to our dominant objective of deterrence. It is, by definition, the first element in NATO's strategy of the flexible response, and perhaps above all it is essential, in the words of Dr. Schlesinger, the United States Secretary for Defense in the early 1970s, 'to build up and maintain a stalwart conventional defense if the nuclear threshold is to be kept high'. The fact of knowing that this balance must be struck, despite the difficulties, does not make the task any easier.

So an attempt will be made here, but before it starts some words are necessary on the general rules to be used. Numbers must of course weigh heavily in the balance, although even these must not be taken at their face value without qualification. There are then two sets of weighting factors necessary to complete (though they will not in themselves solve) the equation. One set may be loosely described as the tangibles to the extent that they can be touched, usually counted and sometimes measured, and the other as the intangibles which cannot—although their manifestations can usually be felt and occasionally even be seen. In the nature of things it is quite normal for the intangibles to attract more disagreement than the tangibles, although there is no unanimity on what are the relative weights of each of these, even among the professionals whose business it is to weigh them. In case the reader is not by now sufficiently confused, the ground rules are complicated by the paradox that we sometimes know more precisely the weight of some of the elements in the Warsaw Pact scale than we do about our own.

So to the numbers game. Before quoting any figures, which in any event tend to glaze the eye, reference must be made to some received wisdom about them. Liddell Hart was the first to propound the notion that in a European war between similarly armed adversaries the attacker would be wise to count upon a numerical superiority of about three to one over the defence before starting. While a different ratio has been shown to have applied in, say, Malaya (about seven to one) or Vietnam (nearer twelve to one), this European norm has never been seriously or successfully challenged and can rely upon some quite extensive historical collateral. This ratio subsumes the inherent advantages of prepared positions, interior lines and so on to the defence, and of the initiatives of time, place and manner in the hands of the attacker. It does not subsume, although the option remains valid, the ability of an attacker to concentrate before an attack, and thus the ratios of men deployed (still similarly equipped) in standing forces is not a suitable basis for estimating whether the critical Liddell Hart level has been reached or not. Respectable authorities have suggested that covert concentration could raise a standing ratio of three to one as high as seven to one locally; or, if the defender is alert and well informed, one may suppose that it could be reduced by the same means to, say, two to one or possibly evens. One begins to apprehend that even without the tangibles and intangibles this is an equation with rather too many variables for comfort, although the prudent would-be balancer could do worse than cling to Liddell Hart.

Taking the elements in the British order of seniority, even though most of the Allies do not, a later chapter will be devoted to the remarkable expansion of Soviet maritime power. In this aspect of the conventional balance it is undoubtedly more difficult to compare numbers on, over and under the sea in a meaningful way, partly because types differ more markedly than they do on land or in the air and partly because the influence of the tangibles and intangibles is generally accepted to be more pronounced. Before dealing with these latter, suffice it to say that NATO navies together outnumber those of the Warsaw Pact (it must be noted and remembered that the Polish and East German navies are far from insignificant). A detailed catalogue would be tedious, and would not contribute much to an understanding of the maritime conventional balance, but the tonnage of the NATO navies is vastly greater, they have six times the number of attack aircraft carriers, and one-and-a-half times the number of ships of frigate size and above. The Warsaw Pact has rather more nuclear-powered attack submarines and at least five times more diesel-engined submarines (though many of these are obsolescent). The Soviet land-based naval air forces are perhaps ten times more numerous than those of NATO, but the reverse is true of those afloat. It must be observed parenthetically that the Liddell Hart yardstick has never been intended to apply to maritime forces, mainly because all the weighting factors which apply to the land–air battle have quite different values in the maritime environment. Finally, the number of men—not that this matters much—deployed in the maritime balance shows a ratio of about seven to four in our favour.

On land the picture is very different. Very briefly, the Warsaw Pact forces are more numerous in all respects. To be slightly more specific, their ground troops are about one-and-a-half times more numerous; their tank advantage is about three to one and the same is true of armoured personnel carriers (though in the air-portable variant it is more like seven to one); in field artillery pieces and bridging equipment one can put their advantage at two to one; and a very much larger advantage is seen in tank transporters. There is another set of comparisons which is commonly made in this class of work, concerning numbers of divisions, regiments, armies and other similarly imprecise terms. These are on the whole value-less today because the composition of such formations now varies so widely, not only between the Warsaw Pact and NATO but between the national forces of both sides, that it is quite impossible in these terms to compare like with like. Even quite experienced operators quickly become confused once they get into 'battle groups', 'regimental combat teams' and the like, and this is why no such comparisons are attempted here.

There is one highly important imbalance—that in chemical warfare shells—which can not be quantified for an entirely different reason. Here we find that a quarter of all the shells deployed by the Soviet Union are designed for this role and the comparable NATO figure is, for practical purposes, nil. Finally there exists a marked difference in the manner in which the land forces are deployed in the Central Region. NATO's forces are, without doubt, mal-deployed in peacetime largely because they are still stationed where they came to rest in 1945. These positions would certainly not have been chosen for any military reason, but it has proved politically impossible and economically out of the question to re-dispose the forces of either Northern or Central Army Group. Some of the former are as much as forty-eight hours from their general defence positions (though mainly for political reasons), and most of the latter are disposed around one of the less likely axes of any armoured advance from the East. By contrast the Warsaw Pact forces, particularly since they have been so significantly augmented in the last few years, are so deployed as to be capable (in military terms) of an advance virtually anywhere along the demarcation line with little or no prior concentration. It is this disadvantage which gives rise to the vexed discussion about 'surprise attack' which will be further discussed in a later chapter. These land force figures do not make cosy reading, but they do not (either in Liddell Hart or commonsense terms) amount to a recipe for disaster, nor do they even justify the amount of hand-wringing that they habitually evoke. Still less must they be allowed to justify the foolish ignorance of them which must be attributed to those who seek to reduce NATO's military forces. What does seem to be fair comment is that these ratios, all in favour of the Warsaw Pact, and their shape, would hardly seem necessary for defensive purposes.

Much the same can be said of the air forces on either side of the boundaries of Allied Command Europe. In this element straight numerical comparisons are particularly unhelpful in striking the balance, because the tangibles of—for example—age, type, weapon fit and role, and the intangibles of doctrine and state of training and control, count for much more. These will be dealt with next. For the insistent numerologist it must suffice to say that the Warsaw Pact has a standing-force superiority of between one-and-a-half and two to one in aircraft. Surface-to-air missiles can, in principle, be counted as either land or air forces—which is a favourite subject for enjoyable disagreement among those who might enjoy debating how many angels can dance upon the head of a pin. It has also, more tiresomely, consumed a vast amount of highly paid time and energy during the negotiations in Vienna about force reductions, which began in October 1973 and still continue. For the present purposes they will be counted as air forces, and we find in this important area a Warsaw Pact advantage of about ten to one. A comparison of manpower in this element means as little as it does at sea, but for completeness we find here, rather surprisingly, a NATO advantage of about two to one.

It is now time to look at the tangibles, and to start by saying what are the most important of them in this balance. Equipment obviously comes high on the list, and close behind it what is usually described, in a generic sense, as support. These two are probably of the same importance but they attract a quite different amount of attention in the general debate, which is a pity. This is explained by the general feeling that guns, missiles, lasers, tanks, bombs, supersonic aircraft and, in a darkly sinister way, submarines are more exciting to see and touch and talk about and write about than great piles of boots or bullets, or beef, or large oil installations, or workshops or caterpillar excavators—as indeed they are. If beauty and excitement are in the eye of the beholder, sheer hard practical utility is what turns on the Commander or his planner. Thus each of these groups of tangibles should carry about the same weight in the balance we are seeking to strike. The essential features of equipment which must be compared are function, age, reliability in the hands of troops under adverse climatic and environmental conditions, and performance in terms of accuracy, damage potential, range, speed of action or reaction, transportability and several others.

It must be borne in mind that cost, or rather production constraints, which in general are of great importance, are only so in this context in so far as they limit or influence the above criteria in other ways. How, then do NATO and the Warsaw Pact measure up in the important comparison of the quality of their kit? Scholarly monographs could and should be written on this subject, but such attempts as have been made have all been either too narrow or too superficial to help us much on the broad front. Fortunately there is little informed disagreement with the over-simplified view that NATO equipment is better than that of the Warsaw Pact, because it can be seen that the technological base which has given it birth is, on both sides of the Atlantic, more highly developed, more diverse and more imaginative, and the engineering of it for production is more sophisticated, than the same factors in the East. This quality gap to the advantage of the West has, throughout NATO's lifetime, been greatly relied upon to redress the quantitative superiority of the Warsaw Pact already described. It may be noted here that this extremely important advantage and counter-poise is now being eroded by the speed with which Soviet quality is improving—this will be dealt with at some length in a later chapter as one of the more important of NATO's current problems.

Advantage in terms of support is less easy to assess. However bright and shiny your equipment, and however well it measures up to all the criteria of efficient deterrence, it will soon run out of gas or ammunition, it will soon need maintenance or overhaul, it will need repair if it is damaged, it has to be brought to where the action is, and it has to be able to receive and understand and comply with instructions about what to do when it gets there. It may even have to be replaced if put out of action and certainly protected so that it is not. The men who do all these things for it have to be fed and watered; they also have to be protected, and they also need repair and replacement. These are the functions of support, and it is worth looking rather more closely at one of them, after noting that the short and simple word 'support' embraces the whole enormous field of logistics, stocks and transport, supply and re-supply, reserves and reinforcement, the apparatus of command and control, and the communications without which the whole enterprise of war would almost immediately collapse. It also embraces passive defence, including hardened headquarters, aircraft and personnel shelters, not only for the teeth arms but also for what has often been poetically described as the man behind the gun, or the man behind him. What is quite beyond argument is that bright and shiny equipment manned by battleworthy and dedicated men is not going to frighten or deter a potential aggressor, unless he can perceive that all these components of support are also in the order of battle. If the words 'Don't start something you can't finish' should be pinned above every Commander's desk (and over his Minister's too), then only the logistician can provide the means by which the same Commander can be sure of finishing the business he (or his Minister) started.

Reinforcement demands a closer look, not because it is the most important support function but because it bears more directly on the numbers game, and more obviously on the balance, than do the others. As will be seen in a later chapter about the special problems of each Region, NATO depends far more on reserves for battle-readiness than does the Warsaw Pact, and it also depends on reinforcement to complete its order of battle. This is mainly because its Allies are doggedly united in their unreadiness to meet the cost of full-strength, in-place forces in either social or financial terms. In all NATO countries reserve forces exist, although their terms of service, competence, equipment and numbers vary widely from country to country. In a rough and ready way, the full mobilisation of NATO's reserves would approximately double Allied manpower, but a distinction must be drawn between these people and the problem of getting them to their General Defence Positions, and those who comprise the reinforcement forces and the quite different problem of getting them to where their Commanders judge they are needed. Both are complicated exercises in logistics, and each demands very tight planning which must be closely co-ordinated with a host of civil agencies who, on the whole, are not accustomed to and do not much like this sort of work. But it has to be done, and well done, if our deterrent posture is to make sense to our own people, quite apart from its effect on a potential aggressor. To give an example of what this is all about, one need only reflect that more than 50,000 men and women have to be sent from the United Kingdom to Germany to bring Rhine Army up to its full war strength; and they will travel by car and train, by sea and air, and complete the journey by road or rail to distribution points in Germany. This sort of problem is repeated to a greater or lesser extent along the whole 2,000-mile length of NATO's eastern boundary, and is a different aspect of our mal-deployment, mentioned earlier.

To get reserves or reinforcements to destinations for which they are earmarked in advance, contingency plans can be made in slow time and practised and improved and kept well-oiled and ready, but the survival of some section of a potential front, if fighting had started, would certainly depend upon such plans actually working on the day of the race. And this must be perceived by both sides if deterrence is to remain valid. All these factors apply equally to the different type of plans for getting the types of reinforcement which are not earmarked in advance to where, in a time of rising tension or crisis, Commanders decide they are most urgently needed. These must be well-oiled too, but in the nature of things can not be so frequently or readily or convincingly practised. Bearing in mind that reinforcing forces can be men or machines or both, from sub-unit to formation level, from North America or from next door, in sea, land or air elements, it must be apparent without further emphasis that reinforcement is very close to the heart of our military posture and thus an almost discrete element in the conventional balance.

The Warsaw Pact has a reinforcement problem too, although it is different in degree. Their forces are kept at a higher peace establishment than those of NATO, and for this and other reasons at a shorter notice to move. Their reinforcements of land and air forces are numerous, but much, although not all, of their kit is held in the forward areas. They also have the classic advantages of operating on interior lines, under single control and with standardised equipment and doctrine. In all these circumstances our logisticians would be very happy to exchange problems with theirs, even though the latter also are not inconsiderable. Some indication of the importance which attaches to this in the Soviet Union, and of their determination to improve in all military matters, is given by the six-monthly routine troop rotations to their western forward areas. Typically, about 140,000 men are moved each way. In 1970 nearly all went by rail and the process took six weeks, but in 1976 more than 120,000 were moved by air, some 90 per cent of the total, and the operation was finished in fourteen days, using Aeroflot capacity without any apparent reduction in the airline's normal services. Although not relevant to the reinforcement problem as such, nor thus to the conventional balance, this is as good a place as any to remark that if, during this airborne routine troop rotation, the aircraft returned to the east empty, we should not know for some time, and a highly significant addition could be made covertly in this way to their order of battle.

It is not necessary to devote much time to the other tangibles, not because they are less important in the spectrum of contributions to the conventional balance but because their function is implicit in their name. Passive defence is a much discussed and well-understood affair and has been the thesis for more than one doctorate, describing, for example, the rate of exchange between aircraft shelters and surface-to-air missiles or air superiority fighters, and opening up fascinating side avenues for disagreement about the trade-off between the hardness of such shelters and the efficacy and relative 'smartness' of missiles designed to destroy them. For the purpose of discussing the conventional balance here, it should be sufficient to say that all Soviet and most non-Soviet Warsaw Pact combat aircraft are permanently in shelters, but that less than three-quarters of NATO's smaller total numbers are so fortunate. Our perceived deterrence is therefore diminished to that extent.

The last tangible which is very much worth a mention is the apparatus for command, control and communication (frequently written, in American, as C3). The place of these interlocking elements in the military scene has been established, discussed and accepted since before the time of Christ. In short, if a Commander has not got them, or if they are not good enough for his strategy (and maybe his tactics too), then he will almost certainly fail. That their level of sophistication has grown from a strong runner with a forked stick (Marathon?) to an immensely complicated and expensive system, founded on electronic automation working at the very frontiers of this new discipline and made in some of the most advanced factories in the world, and with their 'software' a lifetime career for Ph.D.s, is neither here nor there. In any future war, he who cannot communicate upwards, downwards and sideways, sufficiently quickly and sufficiently surely, cannot win—this time it is the literal truth. The aspect of C3 which weighs in the conventional balance is that the West is better at it, not only because of the technological advantage which we still hold (and in this matter the European track record is at least as good as that in North America) but because we need to be better. We need to be better because our style of command and control is infinitely more flexible and is exercised through communication not only at the top but several levels, or layers, lower than it is in the East. The highly centralised control of Warsaw Pact forces, and their much greater reliance on the rigid observance of doctrine and pre-conceived plans, reduces the need for communications at the political level and in the military networks alike. It will be seen that we have entered a grey area between tangibles and intangibles, which provides a good opportunity to look at some of the latter and say a little more about the notion, rather than the means, of communication to be found there.

Those political and military elements which count in the conventional balance but which cannot be touched, measured or quantified weigh no less heavily on that account. However, their values in the scales are, by their nature, inevitably based more on opinion and judgement. The most important, not in any particular order of priority, are generally agreed to be the state of training, morale, leadership in the strictly military sphere, and the availability and quality of intelligence which is part of the linkage between the military intangibles and the more directly political ones such as warning time and the use to be made of it (to be discussed in more detail in Chapter XI on Crisis Management), passive defence and political will.

The state of training, which is of equal importance whether one is considering the individual, his unit or his formation, is likely—because of what are really social or ideological pressures—to differ much more in NATO's forces than in those of the Warsaw Pact. An important determinant is the length of conscript service, which is standard in the East and stated to be two years, but varies in NATO from long-service career men, typically serving as much as twenty years or more, to certain countries where it has been reduced, entirely for socio-political and not for military reasons, to as little as eight months. Senior NATO officers are unlikely to dissent from the view that for land forces about eighteen months is the minimum period in which a soldier can learn the basic essentials of formation fighting, and eight is probably just about enough to make him safe among his friends in a sub-unit, say at platoon level. For the sailor and airman, even in these days when their jobs are much more narrowly specialised in the junior ranks, most Admirals and Air Force Generals would insist upon a minimum of two years or even more. These figures are naturally subject to some weighting by the reserve liability, which varies from one NATO country to another, and plainly it will be difficult to equate an eight-month conscript who then serves for five years in the reserve, and who while doing so actually trains for six weeks each year, with another who may do fifteen months with the colours followed by only two weeks' training a year. The professional competence of each will also be directly affected by such things as the quality of his instructors, the modernity or otherwise of his kit, the amount of live firing in which he takes part, and so on. As a sweeping generalisation, but likely to be somewhat more accurate than most such broad brush strokes, it is almost certainly true that the conscripts (but not career men) are likely to be more competent as individual professionals in the Eastern armies than in those of NATO, but because of their different structure the reverse is probably true of the navies and air forces.

Whether these individuals make up better or worse teams at unit or formation level depends on other factors, of which training in the sense of exercises is one of the most important. The manner in which these are devised and conducted reflects rather accurately (perhaps this is not surprising) the very clear difference in philosophy between the two Alliances. The Warsaw Pact forces are under very tight central control and direction, and initiative is not encouraged. While NATO has certainly based itself on central control and direction, it is much looser, and initiative right down to sub-unit level is actively encouraged. Thus Warsaw Pact exercises, on almost every scale, are much more set-pieces than the free-play within a general scenario which characterises those of NATO. So far as this affects the balance, these comparisons would lead to the conclusion that if everything goes according to plan, the Warsaw Pact might have the edge, but if it did not, then certainly NATO would have it. So it is agreeable for us to remember that, historically, battles and even wars hardly ever have gone according to plan.

It is difficult to be any more precise than this about leadership and morale, favourite subjects though both have always been in almost any discussion of military matters. What has just been said about philosophy probably reads across to these two intangibles as well. It may at least be supposed that because NATO is by definition a defensive Alliance, our armed forces will be defending not only their way of life (which is not perhaps the dominant thought in the minds of individuals should battle actually be joined) but their homelands and their families (which almost certainly is). So their morale should be higher, and their motivation keener, than the morale and motivation of those sent forth in pursuit of an idelogy with which, it is at least arguable, not all of them are deeply in love—which allows at least a reasonable doubt as to whether the non-Soviet Warsaw Pact forces will be wholly reliable. This, in passing, must be taken into account by those who still prefer to strike their balance on the basis of numbers; it is certainly not to be discounted that if, for example, Hungarian, Czech or Polish formations are unreliable, some significant number of the Soviet forces may have to be deployed to keep an eye on them. Much the same arguments as affect morale must be expected to apply to leadership, so long as it is borne in mind that while it is tempting to believe that democratic officers and NCOs are, by some natural law, better leaders than those in a closed society, this would be a highly suspect basis for planning or policy.

Intelligence (with a capital 'I'), like communications, has always been at the heart of military matters, but it cannot be measured any more easily. It may be assumed that the collection facilities on each side are broadly similar in a technical sense, and thus it is the use which each side makes of intelligence which should be compared; this too is likely to differ as the philosophies differ. The NATO policy is, in principle, that all concerned should know as much as possible about what is going on, and it can be surmised, on a certain amount of hard evidence, that dissemination of intelligence and even infor-mation is less in quantity in the East and goes much less far down the line. It is just possibly relevant that in the Red Army at company level only the Commander has a map but it is perhaps too facile, and even unfair, to suggest that this is because he is the only man in the company who can read one. So perhaps we may conclude that strategic information is available in about equal measure to both high commands, but that more use is likely to be made of it, with the consequent advantages in tactics as well as in strategy, by NATO.

To complete the catalogue of intangibles, and thus those leading elements of all kinds which affect the balance, political will must be listed as a primary if not the absolutely dominant term in the equation. This has been mentioned before and will be mentioned again, for there is hardly one aspect of NATO business, certainly not one aspect of deterrence, in which it is not of supreme importance. In the strict sense of this chapter about the conventional balance, it is likely to be most manifest—or to be lacking—in the extent to which use is made of warning time. The will to allocate sufficient resources to create a conventional military machine which can be put in this balance at all is, for the moment and for this purpose, taken for granted. As the description of reserves and reinforcement has attempted to make clear, NATO's order of battle, unlike that of the Warsaw Pact, is kept in peacetime well below war establishment. It can only be brought to a General Defence posture by the accretion of its reserves and the increased readiness of its reinforcements, and these can only be made available by political decision. Thus by what should be a happy chance but is more frequently seen to be a desperately difficult matter of judgement, one of the clearest demonstrations of political will is the very act of bringing our military forces to short notice and thus enhancing deterrence.

Rather in the same way as it is impossible to prove that there is or is not a threat, so is it impossible to prove precisely where the pointer on the scales of the conventional balance rests today. This chapter has sought to explain why this is so and to set out several of the very large number of factors which must be taken into account in the search for what can only be a value judgement. Opinions about it have differed widely, especially in recent years, and will no doubt continue to do so. By no means all the opinions expressed have been objective, the bias of some being political, of others economic, of others national or industrial or both, and several nakedly springing from the wish to grind an axe of one sort or another. On so serious a matter these special pleadings really will not do, particularly if they are presented as either horror stories or fairy stories, and only the best informed judgement in the light of all the factors is likely to lead to a sound basis for future policy.

In this spirit it must be very difficult to dissent from the view that the pointer must now read somewhere fairly close to 'satisfactory'—otherwise this book would neither have been written nor be read. What is more important is to watch rather closely for any signs that the pointer is moving one way or the other, and to consider what action is necessary to keep it in the right place. This is a different exercise, though it is of equal or greater importance. Because the evidence shows unmistakably that the conventional scales are tilting to NATO's disadvantage, it will be dealt with separately in Chapter XIV, 'The Way Ahead'.

CHAPTER V

THE NUCLEAR DILEMMA

Nuclear affairs have, not surprisingly, attracted very wide attention since the first elementary nuclear weapon was dropped on Hiroshima in August 1945. They have been, and still are, the subject of a worldwide debate spanning the spectrum of the emotional, religious, political, moral, economic and, less frequently, military considerations. A good deal of this debate has not been particularly well informed, some of it is factually incorrect, and regrettably little is truly objective. This is unfortunate, because nuclear arms are different in kind and not in degree from all other weapons systems, and it is correspondingly important to understand in which respects this difference arises, and what is really at stake, when their use is discussed.

To inform this debate, and to put this comparatively new engine of war in its correct place in the whole ladder of deterrence upon which our security rests, it is necessary briefly to review the evolution of these weapons in basic military and, above all, political terms. Following the Second World War, while the West demobilised and then began re-building, it was the strategic nuclear superiority of the United States that kept the Soviets in check. In the 1950s, the strategy of massive nuclear retaliation provided the necessary umbrella of security for NATO. But in the 1960s, with the massive deployment of Soviet nuclear missiles shifting the super-power balance towards parity and finally arriving there, it became clear that this strategy would have to be altered. The 'all or nothing' philosophy became less credible as a deterrent to all forms of attack as the Soviet capability to respond in kind became more apparent. In the late 1960s, NATO moved into the strategy of flexible response—that is, a military response graduated to the provocation (the French call it '*la riposte graduée*'). No longer

43

should there be a 'trip-wire' that would provoke a massive nuclear response, but NATO's political leaders could choose from a number of options ranging from purely conventional defence, through controlled escalation of the conflict, including the selective (so-called tactical) use of nuclear weapons, to all-out nuclear war.

In an era of broad strategic nuclear parity, deterrence to every form of aggression cannot be based upon strategic nuclear forces alone; and for this reason NATO strategy calls for a balanced force structure of interdependent strategic nuclear, theatre nuclear and conventional force capabilities. In this Triad, each leg (the purists say that Triads do not have legs and prefer 'element') performs a unique role; in combination, they provide mutual support and reinforcement. The strategic nuclear forces are composed of land, sea and air systems of intercontinental range (ICBMs), and today only the United States and the Soviet Union have massive ICBM capabilities.

Some rather detailed account of the various elements must be given if the magnitude of the whole ICBM enterprise is to be appreciated and the very real difficulties of controlling its proliferation understood. As expected, the Soviets have continued to expand and modernise all elements of their nuclear arsenal, but their qualitative improvements have been more extensive, more diverse and quicker than was at first anticipated. Turning first to ICBMs, the Soviets are ahead in numbers of launchers—1,054 for the United States compared with nearly 1,500 for the Soviets who also enjoy a substantial advantage in warhead megatonnage (total explosive power) while the United States, on the other hand, has the advantage in accuracy, and for the present in multiple re-entry vehicle (MIRV) technology, and thus has more warheads. But the present American lead in both of these areas may prove to be transitory, in view of the determined Soviet efforts which are apparent to deploy MIRVed warheads and to improve their accuracy.

In the 1970s, the Soviets have introduced four new ICBMs into their inventory, three of which are known to have MIRV capability—the SS–17, –18 and –19. The fourth ICBM, the SS–X–16, has not yet been deployed operationally, but it could be very shortly and it could be deployed in a mobile mode. The United States is developing advanced technology for a new ICBM, at present designated 'MX', which could be deployed in a ground or mobile mode, and is intended to provide a hedge against Soviet momentum and other uncertainties in the strategic environment in the 1980s.

The Soviets also have a significant lead in numbers of submarine-launched ballistic missiles—880 to 656 for the United States. Two new Soviet SLBMs are under development—the SS–NX–17 and SS–NX–18—both of which are in the flight test stage of development, which is expected to last another year. The –17 has been observed with only a single re-entry vehicle, but the presence of a post-boost vehicle lends credence to the possibility that it will later be MIRVed. This and the –18 will probably be deployed on a variant of the Delta class ballistic missile submarine (SSBN).

While the Soviets stretch their Delta class submarines to accommodate new missiles, the United States is going forward with the Poseidon programme; it is converting thirty-one of its forty-one fleet submarines for this programme and is continuing work on the Trident system which should be operational in 1979. The United Kingdom augments the American capability with four Polaris SSBNs, and the French have four of similar performance but separately controlled.

The Soviets currently have a mix of some 265 long-range turboprop Bear and turbojet Bison aircraft. It is believed that approximately 140 of these are permanently configured for use in the strategic nuclear bomber role, though many of the others could be similarly adapted. The most controversial aircraft now operational in the Soviet inventory is the Backfire, and it is difficult to say how many have already been deployed; it is probably more than fifty, with the build-up expected to continue. The Soviets contend that this is an intermediate-range system and therefore does not fall into the strategic category, even though the Backfire is capable of in-flight refuelling which would enable it to achieve intercontinental range. Nevertheless, the Alliance still has the edge in the bomber category with a mix of some 500 United States B–

52s and FB–111s, the Vulcans of United Kingdom Strike Command, and the French Mirages in a different category.

From the foregoing, it could be held that a rough parity in strategic systems now exists, and that the West retains the ability to deter a disarming Soviet first strike. The margin is less pronounced than it was only a few years ago, as the Soviets inch forward in developing MIRVed ICBMs and SLBMs, their improved Delta class SSBNs, and the introduction of the Backfire, which adds another term to the strategic equation and must therefore be taken into account, whether the Russians like or not (which they don't).

When attempting to assess the balance of theatre nuclear forces, the sheer numbers of different kinds of weapons and delivery systems makes this a formidable and, outside military or civilian centres for strategic studies, an unexciting task. Aircraft, artillery, medium and intermediate range ballistic missiles (IRBMs), gravity bombs, atomic demolition munitions and air defence weapons should all be taken into account even though their functions and performances differ so widely. The Soviets have tested a new IRBM, the SS–X–20, which is known to be both mobile and MIRVed, and could be deployed operationally at any time; indeed, this has almost certainly begun. It is believed that it is intended to replace many of the existing IRBMs, the SS–4s and –5s, which would quadruple the present number of such warheads. The Soviets have also pressed on vigorously to improve their battlefield nuclear weapons, namely the Scud, Frog and Scaleboard systems, and it is highly probable that they possess artillery with a nuclear capability. Soviet tactical and nuclear-capable aircraft have undergone improvements in recent times which have sub-stantially improved range, payload and electronic warfare capabilities. The most dramatic improvement witnessed is their increasing ground attack capability (conventional as well as nuclear), which has enabled their tactical air forces to engage in a broader range of offensive missions—in particular, the capability to conduct strikes against most of NATO's airfields without prior re-deployment. The foregoing improvements and advances by the Soviets are sobering indeed, but they are being met by the introduction of new nuclear-capable aircraft for the

Alliance, such as the European Jaguar and MRCA, and the American F-15 and F-16. The US Lance surface-to-surface missile and an improved Pershing also play an important part in our theatre weapons systems inventory, as well as their improved 8-inch Howitzer shell which, together with the 155mm. projectile, make up NATO's nuclear artillery stockpile. To these American weapons, made available under the 'two-key' system to the European Allies as well, must be added the French Pluton surface-to-surface nuclear missile and the French and British theatre nuclear bombs. In assessing this diverse theatre nuclear balance, it may be said in the most general way that NATO today retains the edge in quality and in numbers, but it must be recognised that the Soviets probably have at least equal momentum. Extraordinary efforts will therefore be required to maintain NATO's historic qualitative advantage in this field.

If this very brief and deliberately over-simplified analysis is broadly accepted, it must also be clear that a visible, responsive and versatile theatre nuclear capability is indispensable to successful deterrence and defence, and provides a vital rung on the ladder of escalation. It is worth reminding ourselves frequently just what we are talking about in this shorthand, since the readily labelled 'tactical' or 'theatre' nuclear weapons now deployed by all the nuclear powers have, typically, yields of ten or more times those of the only two such devices so far used in anger—those dropped on Hiroshima and Nagasaki. Far too few who talk and write so glibly about these ghastly devices remember this, or give adequate thought to what will be going on in the mind of a possible recipient. It has always seemed to me a bizarre notion to suppose that this unfortunate individual will recognise that what has just vaporised him and square miles of his surroundings, and perhaps a million of his friends, was 'just' a tactical nuclear weapon.

So let it never be forgotten that nuclear weapons, of whatever yield, are just that—nuclear weapons. They may be used for intercontinental bombardment or in-theatre in a tactical situation, but the essential fact is that they represent a quantitative and qualitative change in the nature of warfare. They are not simply an extension of conventional weaponry, regardless of their accuracy or yield; so let us put away once and for all the thought that the so-called 'mini-nukes' or weapons the size of cricket balls are less provocative or diminish the possibility of nuclear escalation, once the nuclear threshold is crossed.

The public debate on this possibility has been sharpened by the technical feasibility of the United States deploying enhanced radiation weapons, the so-called 'neutron bomb'. This has attracted as much debate, on almost as many levels, as the whole question of nuclear weapons, but equally, and regrettably, little of it has been truly objective and hardly any of it well-informed. There are even those proponents of the contraption who put it about that these are not really nuclear weapons at all, but, as with tactical nuclear weapons, whether they or anyone at the receiving end would continue to hold this view after it had been used would seem, at the least, dubious—perhaps as dubious as the likelihood of another nuclear power deciding to regard them as non-nuclear weapons. At the other end of the poetic (or semantic) scale are those who hold that they are as nuclear as an intercontinental ballistic missile. Most uncommitted observers might agree that, of the two views, the second is nearer to the truth.

Let us reduce the debate to very simple terms. Herman Kahn in his book *On Escalation*, published in 1965, said: 'Once war has started, no other line of demarcation is at once so clear, so sanctified by convention, so ratified by emotion, so low on the scale of violence and—perhaps most important of all—so easily defined and understood as the line between using and not using nuclear weapons.' And a nuclear weapon is a nuclear weapon and the 'neutron bomb' is a nuclear weapon. If it is used, Kahn's line will have been crossed.

Other examples of new technology have been much in the forefront in the recent past, and while not an overall panacea for Alliance weaknesses, it will certainly play a vital role in the years ahead. Improved sensors, integrated micro-circuits, propulsion technologies and laser applications all offer a new range of possibilities. We should not expect these improvements to be cheap—they are not. It is a truism that for any major weapon a follow-on system of the same type will be significantly more expensive, and this is as true of nuclear weapons as it is of conventional ones. Let us look rather more closely at two of the most important nuclear weapons systems which have been made possible by this rolling back (forward?) of the frontiers of technology. There is, conveniently, one such system either in, or capable of being added to, the inventory of each super-power.

On the Soviet side there is the mobile intermediate range (by which is implied less than intercontinental) ballistic missile, the SS–X–20, which was mentioned in the catalogue. This beast does not fit tidily into the normally comprehended bracket of weapons which can be used to bombard at very long range, nor of those which are intended for use on the battlefield or for interdiction not too far behind it. It has at least three other awkward characteristics, which alone would merit some special attention. If launched from Warsaw Pact territory, it would be sure to land on European heads, but no negotiating machinery exists (certainly not at present) into which the Europeans could register their dislike of this fact or through which they could engage in a dialogue leading to some control of its use. Even those who believe it is a 'strategic' weapon (a difficult view to rebut) can see no way to include discussion of it, by its potential recipients, in the bilateral talks on the limitation of strategic arms between the super-powers. Its mobility presents an almost purely military problem, equally intractable in that to neutralise it quickly enough is technically very difficult.

On our side the United States is developing long-range Cruise missiles. Essentially, these weapons are small, extremely accurate unmanned aircraft, subsonic in speed and able to penetrate defences at low altitudes, which makes their detection by radar very difficult—and usable in either a conventional or nuclear mode. They may, technically, be launched from platforms on land, in the air, and on or under the sea.

In the nuclear mode these weapons have naturally attracted much attention either as a demonstration of the (undoubted) technological superiority of the United States, or as a counter to the Russian SS–X–20 (which is dubious), or as an easy but long stride towards redressing the pace at which the Soviets are eroding the lead of the Americans in intercontinental weapons.

But it is perhaps in ways other than the purely technological
that it needs well-informed and dispassionate study.

First, there are some philosophical aspects of this manifestation of very high technology to deal with. Is it, for example, a
strategic weapon and thus to be part of the long-sought and
eagerly-desired package of SALT II? The Soviets have made it
totally clear that they think so, but from the point of view of
NATO this is a matter for the United States Administration,
which does not. On any view, this missile, apart from its
military potential, is plainly a high card at the political poker
table. What is its weight in the super-power equation? What
is its place in the ladder of escalation? To what extent does it
contribute to the primary objective of Allied deterrence? If
this fails, where does (better, would) it fit into the plans for
war-fighting? These are important and even possibly urgent
questions and, as so often happens, they are very difficult to
answer. And to deal with them thoroughly would also require
a work on its own, although very likely the work would be
overtaken by the remorseless speed of events before, in book-
form at any rate, it could reach lasting conclusions.

What cannot be denied is that the Cruise missile has attracted
a great deal of discussion, and has been one of the most
intractable subjects of disagreement between the Americans
and the Soviets in their efforts to conclude satisfactorily the
second round of their Strategic Arms Limitation Talks (SALT
II). Apart from these and its technical features, there are some
other aspects of it which can be said to inform the debate.
There are those who believe that it can make a contribution
towards a deterrent posture below the level of an intercontinental exchange but above the tactical level, and they
suggest that for various reasons of which not the least is the
arrival of the SS–X–20, the deterrent value of 'tactical/theatre'
weapons in Europe is now much diminished. This is a highly
dubious proposition, almost in the 'When did you stop beating
your wife?' class, and a believer would have to believe too many
other highly unlikely propositions before he could embrace that
notion. There are others, or sometimes some of the same
people, who believe that it is the Western answer to the
SS–X–20. This is certainly more attractive, although not really

much more sensible, because it begs all the questions raised by the Soviet mobile IRBM already mentioned, without providing any of the answers.

Some of those who believe either or both of these propositions go on to say that Soviet tactical nuclear weapons are more destructive and longer-ranged than NATO's and this removes the theatre nuclear rung from NATO's ladder of flexible response by controlled escalation. This dual notion is also highly suspect on almost any uncommitted view, because even if the first leg of it were true—which is certainly an unsupported assertion—the second by no means follows.

Nevertheless there are some grains of sense about principles— although they have not been very convincingly articulated— among some of this arguable chaff about details. At least we can agree that the best time to determine the top of the nuclear escalator would be not during the error-prone stress of crisis management at the major disaster level, but before the game had begun. And it would be equally common ground, one may hope, that the Cruise missile has the unique quality (on the Western side) of being able to strike all that part of Europe (traditionally bounded by the Urals) which the Soviet Union and the Warsaw Pact control, without recourse either to vulnerable delivery systems like manned aircraft or the next rung up the ladder of truly strategic weapons. And so it can, and should, be recognised that the Cruise missile has an important place among the arrows in a super-power quiver.

However there is another highly relevant feature of this new device which is of a different nature from its relevance to the super-power equation. Many well-informed observers ask whether this would not be a good idea for the two Western European nuclear powers as well as for the United States. The answer seems to depend, as so often, on the answer to the question 'for what?'. There is no very good case in military terms for adding this weapon to the French or British inventory simply to increase the number of rungs in their ladder of nuclear deterrence. In financial terms it would also be extremely expensive, and no more deterrence could be offered by French or British politicians if they possessed it than now.

On the other hand there is a respectable, indeed strong, case for considering the Cruise missile, presumably in its air- or sea-launched variants, as a replacement for the French and British submarine-launched first-generation strategic nuclear systems. This debate is topical because of the need for replacement of systems which will be life-expired in the latter half of the next decade. Whether the Cruise missile is the best replacement depends on a host of considerations which need not be rehearsed here, but at least it seems feasible, and in a similar cost bracket, and likely to be as effective as any of the other candidates. It is on the fairly small print of cost effectiveness that the decision should properly be made.*

Returning to the general from this lengthy excursion into the particular, this then is the state of play about nuclear weapons affairs in the round, on which informed judgements can be made. It is very far from simple to be certain of the solution to this puzzle which would best serve NATO's needs, although the nuclear threshold, to return briefly to Kahn, is indeed starkly simple. It is, one must suppose, of almost overriding importance in the interests of deterrence and flexible response to dispose of a full quiver of these desperate arrows. But, thus equipped, it is also of overriding importance to keep the nuclear threshold high, very high, because once it is crossed the consequences are incalculable, and there is almost certainly no going back.

---

* Mr. Ian Smart, in an excellent analysis in his book *The British Nuclear Deterrent: Technical Economic and Strategic Issues*, has covered all this fascinating ground very thoroughly and ably, and I am glad to support his conclusions.

CHAPTER VI

THE REGIONAL PERSPECTIVES

The Alliance is managed politically—that is to say it is informed, controlled, directed and organised—centrally from NATO Headquarters at Evere, just outside Brussels, and by a continuous dialogue between Evere and the national capitals. The integrated military forces are managed in a similar way but commanded by a quite separate military structure to which brief reference has already been made. These central, essentially complementary, arrangements will be described in some detail in a later chapter. This apparently tidy 'organigram' has to take account of the broad sweep of common policies hammered out to meet the common aims of the Treaty which have stood the test of time and the pressure of world events so well that they have remained, in effect, unchanged for many years. But the whole management task also has to take account of some narrower, though no less compelling, constraints and pressures which flow from national identities (some of these are discussed under the heading of 'Family Affairs' in Chapter VIII). There is, besides, another set of influences at work, equally compelling in a different way, brought about by fairly sharp differences in several important respects between the Regions (so designated for command purposes in the first instance). This should come as no surprise in an area which stretches from the North Cape to the Bosporus and from that 2,000-mile-long line westward through the Mediterranean and the North and South Atlantic to the eastern seaboard of North America.

In the Northern Region, which embraces Norway and Denmark, a small but important part of the Federal Republic of Germany, the North and Norwegian seas, and the adjacent waters in the Baltic and its approaches, we find circumstances which demand entirely different treatment from those further south or west. Add to this that, apart from the military convenience of commanding forces in this Region separately, the area is far from homogeneous politically, topographically, economically or in terms of equipment, and it is plain that a puzzle of some complexity is presented to NATO's planners.

Norway has common frontiers with Finland, the Soviet Union and Sweden, and this cannot fail to influence her Government's attitudes in the political field. It is, indirectly if not directly, almost certainly a dominant reason for her refusal to allow foreign troops or nuclear weapons to be stationed on Norwegian soil in peacetime. The happy exploitation of North Sea oil, now well on stream, has vastly improved Norway's economic position—which was not at all bad before— and made available if required very substantial additional resources for defence. It is, in passing, strange to reflect that Norway, almost alone among the NATO Allies, now has more petro-kroner than she can conveniently deal with, and to her credit this has already been reflected in her robust support for the Alliance.

Norway is also a very long and very sparsely populated country, where the difficulties of terrain and climate make north–south communication extremely difficult even by air, and east–west transit only less so because the distances are shorter. The small population means that standing forces must be correspondingly few, and although proportionately large reserve forces exist, these are still small in numbers compared with those in other Regions, and more importantly, than those permanent forces readily available to the Warsaw Pact in Finnmark and the Baltic. These factors of topography and numbers present military planners with another complex puzzle, or perhaps another part of the whole Northern Region puzzle, which the surrounding political constraints make no easier to solve.

Without any further delving into what would make these special problems easier to solve in both political and military terms (the essentials of which require no enormous effort of the imagination), it can be said at once that successful deterrence in Norway depends absolutely critically on our evident ability to reinforce the indigenous forces very quickly. This in turn depends upon highly-geared contingency planning, with unambiguously earmarked forces and supplies and the means of getting them there, and well-organised and highly-trained reception facilities from the host nation. All these elements of demonstrably quick-reaction reinforcement must be frequently and regularly exercised.

Turning further south to the Baltic approaches and Denmark we find some broad similarities in the political considerations, but as many differences. Here there is a very much less favourable economic outlook, and an equally difficult though dissimilar military scenario. Let it be said at once that it has proved impossible, for mainly political reasons, to establish a local command structure, which would be the most efficient from a simply military point of view. Although this is tiresome, it has not—nor should it—loomed too large as a weakness, nor is it worth further tinkering if this would (and surely it would) involve political abrasion.

The essential point about this southerly end of the Northern Region is that the prime requirement for successful deterrence is the same (though the means of achieving it are very different) as it is in Norway, namely a perceived ability for successful rapid reinforcement. The same general criteria also apply to the forces and supplies, and to the means of transport and reception. The complications are, however, of a different nature. By comparison the terrain is less hostile, the distances are shorter, communications are better and points of entry are more numerous and easier of access. But they are also easier of access to an invader, and his route by air or sea across the Baltic is more difficult for the defenders to deny. Perhaps the last problem here is that the area lies close to the hinge between the Northern and Central Region, and is correspondingly more critical in military terms to the integrity of total Allied Defence, although in political terms no geographical part of NATO can, or should, be considered more or less important than any other. These latter factors—but only these—and physical closeness to the hinge are common to the southernmost part of the Northern Region in Schleswig-Holstein. In nearly all other respects this last section is much more like the Central Region, but here, above all, the Northern Region must be seen to be able to hold and to prevent its right flank being turned.

Moving south, we come to the historic European battle-ground which is NATO's Central Region. It is here that massive, well-equipped and superbly trained land and air forces face each other. It is through here that the route to the very heart of Western Europe must pass. It is here that warning time could be very short. It is here that any weakening or failure of conventional arms could most quickly lead to the use of nuclear weapons. It is here that more Allied forces stand together than anywhere else in the NATO area. It is here that command and control and communications and intelligence must be most finely honed. It is here that the great industries of the most powerful European partner, and most of her population, are found. It is here, and almost only here, that the great majority of North American forces are deployed in peacetime. It is here that the balance of conventional forces must be preserved if the nuclear threshold is to be kept high. It is here that the 'French connexion' looms largest (for France as well as for her Allies). It is here that deterrence must be total. For all these reasons, any one of which would be enough by itself, it is upon this Region that the corporate gaze of NATO is continuously focussed.

Whether fighting is most or least likely to start here if it starts at all is certainly arguable. Whether this collective Allied fixation arises from these imperatives, from folk-memories or from the scars of history, and whether it is wise, is neither here nor there. The fact is that for probably a majority of the Allies, the Central Region is the heart of NATO, and in their eyes nothing must be allowed to lessen its health and strength. The outcome of this perception is plain for all to see and, in the absence of some wholly unexpected political development, is highly unlikely to change.

And so southward to Naples where the Commander in Chief of NATO's Southern Region has his Headquarters and, incidentally, has for twenty-five years been the only Admiral at this level of our high command. His problems are as different from those of his opposite number commanding the Central Region at Brunnsum (in peacetime) as they are from those

dealt with for the North at Kølsas. The problems are different
in nature because the political, economic, geographical and
military constraints are all different. Further reference to some
of these will be made later in our excursion round 'Family
Affairs', but some detail is also required here if the complexity
of the total management problem in this area is to be fully grasped.

Without anticipating or extending the discussion of the
political difficulties caused by disagreements between Greece
and Turkey over Cyprus and other matters, the internal
political situations in these countries differ very widely from
those in the other Regions and also from those in Italy. But
numbers of men are not a problem here, as they are in the
North. Greece, Turkey and Italy (and France to the extent
that much of her coast lies in the Southern Region) have very
large numbers of men under arms; to give some perspective
to this assertion, they have together as many men as are
deployed everywhere else in the NATO area. Economic
problems, too, are of a quite different shape, all three countries
being poorer than nearly all the other Allies. Expressed in
another convention, the same three countries are all among the
lowest five of the Allies in the amount spent on defence *per
capita*. Greece and Turkey are among the least industrialised
members and, for this reason as well as for financial ones,
must rely on others for the supply of military equipment—
although this does not apply to anything like the same extent
to Italy. All three countries have a Mediterranean coast with
the attendant hazards and benefits, while Greece and Turkey
share frontiers with the Warsaw Pact, and in Thrace Bulgaria
is only thirty miles from the Aegean Sea. These similarities and
differences not only make the Southern Region's internal
problems difficult but make them quite different from those
encountered to the north.

This Region is also very long, has at least three separate
potential fronts (four if we count the sea), and certainly in its
eastern marches requires reinforcement as urgently as does
the North. It also has, uniquely, on the southern littoral of the
Mediterranean, countries outside both the NATO and Warsaw
Pact Alliances of which some, at least, are likely to be more
inclined to oppose than to support NATO.

Notwithstanding all these intractable problems, it is of the highest importance to the integrity of the Alliance and to the dominant objective of total deterrence, that the political cohesion and its military manifestation should be as reliable and durable here as anywhere else. Sometimes these members of the family feel a little lonely and neglected.

Finally there is, of course, the Atlantic which is not a Region in either the political or the military sense, and where our forces are commanded not by a Major Subordinate Commander but by a Supreme Commander. It would be invidious to suggest that any one Region is more or less important than another, although it might be thought normal for an Admiral of the Fleet, who has spent fifty years on the Active List of the Royal Navy, delicately to suggest that potential threats in these waters are more important to the Alliance than those on land. On the whole (not only in this context) this sailor has spent too long at the top of all three Services to be as parochial as that, but he believes that history and the facts of life speak louder than special pleading. History can be read elsewhere, and will show that while battles can be won and lost in the air and on land as well as on and under the sea, wars may well be won on land but almost never (certainly in modern times) by a side which has lost control of the sea.

So what are the maritime facts? They are simple and daunting. The European Allies depend on the safe and timely arrival by sea of most of their energy, most of their food and most of their raw materials and the subsequent safe and timely arrival, also by sea, of those products of their industries which are exported. The implications of this statement of fact hardly need analysis. They amount, briefly, to saying that in peacetime the NATO Europeans depend for their whole way of life on uninterrupted, two-way, secure sea lines of communication. The degree of this dependence does not depend on the precise or even the rough proportions of the energy, food and raw materials imported or of the manufactures exported. People who do not wish to accept or face the facts like to argue about these proportions, to promote the notion of future self-sufficiency, and to postulate fairy stories about future energy sources independent of black oil, but the honest and thoughtful

ones among them must know that this is silly talk. If the least
alarming figures are chosen (and they are, actually, much too
low), then Western Europe imports about three-quarters of its
energy and raw materials and half its food. There simply is
not any way by which these could be replaced, and by which
our way of life could remain unchanged, if the free passage of
such supplies by sea were to be interrupted. To a considerably
lesser extent the North American Allies are in (perhaps, more
precisely, dependent upon) the same boat, but even our most
powerful member, the United States, is no longer self-sufficient
in energy or raw materials; and the need to preserve this lifeline
is the fact about the Atlantic Region which dwarfs all the
others. It will, regrettably, not go away however much we
determine not to look at it.

From this flows, without any further blinding glimpses of
what should be the obvious, our utter dependence upon, and
the overriding importance of, the Atlantic (as well as the
Channel, the North and Norwegian Seas and the Mediterranean) in times of peace as well as times of tension or, if
deterrence fails, of war. It is not only NATO's people who may
starve, or that the machines on which their military equipment
depend may grind to a halt, but that the only line along which
reinforcement, supply and re-supply can reach Europe from
North America is at risk. This should wonderfully concentrate
our collective mind on what Captain Mahan called 'the
influence of sea power'.

These relatively few words are enough to sketch the job of the
Supreme Allied Commander, Atlantic (SACLANT), in this
fourth Region of NATO, although they do not attempt to
describe the total maritime problem, or to spell out the serious
gaps in NATO's ability to solve it. But so important is this
'sea-affair', as Churchill called it, that the following chapter is
devoted to a detailed examination of Soviet Maritime Expansion, to dispel any lingering doubt of the potential threat which
the Alliance must deter in the 'sea-region', if all its efforts in all
the other Regions are not to be stillborn.

CHAPTER VII

SOVIET MARITIME EXPANSION

For the reasons given in the preceding chapter, and because the expansion of Soviet maritime power has had such a dramatic effect on the super-power relationship in particular, and the world balance of power in general, it is necessary to this analysis of NATO to establish what has happened, why it all began and what the outcome of it is today, and might be in the future. Even without these compelling reasons it is a fascinating success story, worth telling in its own right.

Before attempting the immediate task as it affects this narrative, one needs to look quite a long way back. In Mother Russia, over many centuries, the Romanovs and their Boyars had no maritime aspirations. There were maritime projects in the time of Peter the Great, also known as Peter the Shipwright, and again during the nineteenth century; but nothing that was sustained, and nothing remotely approaching a design for dominion over the oceans, or even indeed any effective control of their confined coastal waters in Europe and Asia. This is not to say that the Tsars had no territorial ambitions; even the most cursory glance shows how, from the basically tribal conglomeration of the sixteenth century, there evolved an empire which successfully engulfed its hitherto independent border-states, in a process which continued successfully right up to the middle of the twentieth century.

The inhabitant of the Russian or Soviet Empire, whatever his ethnic origins, has in the past regarded himself as essentially a land animal and even today it would be true to say that a great majority of the population of the Soviet Union have never seen the sea, have no desire or opportunity to do so, and would not, if they thought about it, regard the Soviet Navy as playing a vital part in the defence (the word needs emphasis) of their country. Nor, historically, have they any naval traditions to look back on; the Imperial Navy was humiliated in the fiasco of Tshushima (Port Arthur), where its numerically superior fleet was annihilated by the Japanese. The mutinies of 1905 and 1917 saw Red sailors in the van of the revolutionary movements, because they despised their officers and because they were basically artisans and peasants who had been pressed into military service in a totally alien environment. The Soviet Navy played virtually no part in the Second World War, and even when British losses in convoys to Russia were becoming critical, such Soviet warships as there were seldom left Murmansk.

The object of starting this passage with a brief reference to the distant past is twofold. First, to illustrate that the popularly held view that the Russians, both historically and by their nature, have never been an imperialistic or expansionist nation is a fallacy. Indeed, ever since the foundation of the Romanov dynasty in 1613, Russia has progressively and successfully pursued a policy of domination of minorities and of absorbing them and their territories into an autocratic empire.

The second purpose in looking so far back is to point out that because NATO in the west and China in the east have so far successfully deterred any further incursions on land, the only fresh option left to the Soviets, if they were not to abandon their aim of world-wide Communisation, was to further their overseas policies by the projection of naval power.

A hundred or so years ago, a nation aspiring to build a navy needed only a few thousand oak trees, a mile or two of canvas and a few foundries, and within a year or two it was in business. In the technological and scientific environment of the latter half of the twentieth century, the process of building a navy takes at least ten, and possibly fifteen years. Even if one considers only the material requirements of the day and disregards the vastness of the manpower and other resources involved, it is apparent that the consequent drain on a national economy, however strong, would be unacceptable in any democratic society, as being quite out of scale with all the competing requirements. So the emergence of the Soviet Navy as we see it today can only have resulted from a deliberate policy, adopted fifteen or more years ago, when far-reaching, enormously costly and quite startling decisions must have been taken, in the knowledge that their full impact on the international scene could not become effective until the 1970s. It is as certain as it can be on the evidence that in about 1960 Admiral Gorschkov read, and finally understood, Captain Mahan's classics on *The Influence of Sea Power*, and that their lessons were indelibly rubbed in to both his heart and mind by the crisis of Cuba in 1962. If ever a deep humiliation had one certain cause it was, quite simply, the fact that the United States commanded the surrounding seas and had the wisdom, courage and determination to make use of that command.

This in itself gives us a glimpse, fleeting perhaps, into the minds of the Soviet leaders, who in taking these decisions must have known with absolute conviction that their expansionist policies would, as a matter of course, be pursued by their successors, and that these policies would eventually demand a naval commitment of massive strength and capability—which is precisely what has emerged. Obviously the first essential for anyone who wishes to start building is to find an architect— and the Soviets had just such a man in the right place at the right time in Admiral Sergei Gorschkov. No discussion about any aspect of the modern Soviet Navy would be complete without some reference to Gorschkov—and it can only be a matter for conjecture to what extent he personally conceived and developed the policy of expansion as well as keeping an iron hand on the deployment of the immense, indeed unlimited, resources placed at his disposal by the Supreme Soviet. This great man is now sixty-nine years old. He entered the navy in 1927 and his career, so far as we know, followed a conventional pattern for a Russian naval officer of his time, except that he became a Rear Admiral at thirty-one, Commander in Chief of the Navy at forty-five, and a member of the Central Committee of the Communist Party in 1956. He survived both the pre- and post-war purges, and one must therefore assume that at no time was he closely associated with any particular faction of the Soviet political hierarchy. In brief, it seems that he concentrated his talents on improving his professionalism—while at the same time mastering the complexities of the technological revolution that were making their impact on maritime affairs—and on introducing the measures that would be necessary to impose these effectively on a navy lacking in the skills and traditions associated with American and European maritime forces. He has done his job—and all the indications are that in the process he has probably groomed successors of the calibre required to sustain the quality of the navy he created, both materially and in the professional attributes necessary to maintain its operations on a worldwide scale.

Against this backcloth to the man himself and his herculean task, it is useful to have Gorschkov's personal definition of what he has achieved and why. In published articles he has said: 'Today we have a fully modern navy, equipped with everything necessary for the successful performance of all missions on the expanses of the world ocean. Naval forces can be used—in peacetime—to put pressure on their enemies, as a type of military demonstration, as a threat to interrupting sea communications, and as a hindrance to ocean commerce. The flag of the Soviet Navy now flies over the oceans of the world. Sooner or later the West will have to understand that it is no longer master of the seas.' He does not, in this passage, refer to war—but that is hardly necessary. He went even further in a recently published book, *The Sea Power of the State*, not available in the West: 'Soviet sea power, merely a minor defensive arm in 1953, has become the optimum means to defeat the imperialist enemy, and the most important element in the Soviet arsenal to prepare the way for a Communised world.' So at least we know where he thinks we all stand.

So let us turn to the point of expansion which the Soviet Navy has reached in its transition from a coastal defence force to the second largest navy in the world. Despite much of what is written and said on this subject in Western circles, to count ships cannot in itself describe or measure a maritime capability. Any balanced assessment must obviously also, and more usefully, take account of the age and performance of the hulls, the variety and quality of their weapons systems, the general state of all the material components and, most important of all, the intangible and unquantifiable factors of the professional competence and dedication of the officers and men. In this context it is beyond doubt that the great majority of ships, submarines and aircraft of the Soviet fleets are comparatively new and in many cases equipped with the most sophisticated and modern weaponry. There is no need to catalogue in detail the numbers and types which make up this formidable fighting force but an assessment of its potential would be incomplete without at least some approximation of both.

In 1976 the Soviets had seventy-eight strategic nuclear-powered submarines with an armoury of 845 strategic nuclear missiles, and eighty-four nuclear-propelled attack submarines, half of them equipped with tactical nuclear missiles. In addition, there were some 150 conventional diesel-propelled submarines, for both operational and training purposes. Their surface forces comprise two Kiev class aircraft carriers in commission with another fitting out, each capable of carrying twenty-five vertical or short take-off and landing (V/Stol) aircraft or large anti-submarine helicopters, or any desired mix of these types. This class is also heavily armed with long- and short-range guided missiles for offensive (surface-to-surface) and defensive (surface-to-air) purposes with a nuclear-headed potential. Coming down the scale of size and power we find two Moskva class helicopter cruisers, sixteen missile-armed anti-submarine cruisers, seven surface-to-surface and surface-to-air missile cruisers, eleven conventional cruisers, eighty destroyers, ninety-seven ocean escorts, and over 1,000 smaller warships of various types. Their fleets are supported by about 150 supply and repair ships, and thus they have become largely self-sufficient in their blue water deployments. Their shore-based naval air force consists of some 650 combat and reconnaissance aircraft, now being enormously enhanced in quality by the Backfire bomber. This is, by the most exacting standards, a very large navy.

It is made even larger if we take account, as we must, of the Soviet fleet's intelligence-gathering arm comprising some fifty vessels, deployed worldwide, although they have no offensive capability in the active sense of the word. There is one further element of this maritime power that must be mentioned. The Soviet Union now has very large and modern merchant shipping, fishing and oceanographical research fleets centrally controlled and directed by the Government. All of these are available at the drop of a hat, and all the time, to be used as instruments of Government policy, either in support of the navy or independently. The research fleet is the largest in the world, the merchant fleet is the world's sixth largest, and many merchant and research vessels have been specifically designed for rapid adaptation to the military support role, as well as having an intelligence-gathering capability.

In addition to numbers and quality, there are two other important considerations which cannot be ignored. First, Soviet surface ships are, in general, more heavily armed and faster than those of other navies. This has been achieved at the expense of the living standards of their crews, who are accustomed at home to a much lower life-style and thus are ready to adapt to cramped and confined quarters which would be unacceptable to our sailors or indeed to those of any enlightened navy in this day and age. The other factor is that the weaponry of the Soviet fleet is now almost entirely oriented towards an offensive role. To those who do not believe this, or do not want to believe it, it must be said that there is no professional to whose satisfaction this has not been demonstrated time and time again during the monitoring of their exercises, and during their encounters with NATO forces, over the past three or four years. Soviet nuclear-powered attack submarines, equipped with anti-ship missiles (with conventional or nuclear warheads) are, if not ahead of the game, certainly front runners, and at present NATO has no comparable forces, nor a really effective counter to their submarine-borne anti-ship missiles. Finally, and very much as an extension of the warship programme, the Soviet naval air force is numerous and modern, well trained and well armed, with an impressive inventory of stand-off missiles. New aircraft and new weapons are continually being introduced into service and there is no doubt that this maritime air force is continuing to expand and to improve in quality.

Finally, in the allocation of the vast resources devoted to military research and development in the Soviet Union, it is evident that the Soviet Navy is given high priority. A very considerable ship- and submarine-building programme is still under way, and the rate of building of nuclear-powered submarines is estimated to be of the order of ten every year. Comparable rates in the United States might be three, and in France and the United Kingdom together, less than two.

To return to the intangible factor of the quality of the officers and men, we can be reasonably sure that the Soviet naval officer is now a well qualified professional. But at all levels there are clear indications of a reluctance to act without direction, specific authority, or at best consultation, and in the tightly-knit chain of command, there is little opportunity for demonstrating initiative or taking even minor decisions. Where the men are concerned, their navy has inflicted on itself by the very ambitious extent of its expansion a vast training programme. The majority of the ratings are three-year conscripts and, extrapolating from Western experience, this must involve manning shortages, particularly in the submarine element. The usage rate (operational days at sea per year) of the Soviet ships tends to be low in comparison with Western navies and this, coupled with the tight control already mentioned, must cast some reasonable doubt on the depth of the competence and experience of both officers and men. This is, of course, something which time can certainly improve, if not cure. While it is of no great significance, it is of interest that many of their officers spend several years in the same ship, and one case is known of a Captain aged thirty-one who had spent all his naval career, apart from shore training courses, in the same ship.

So much, at least for the moment, for the build-up of the Soviet Navy as it is today, on its strength and capabilities, and on its potential as an instrument of an expansionist policy. Let us turn now to the manner in which this Navy is used and deployed, to the facilities which are available to it overseas, and to the sinister undertones of its almost inevitable appearance or reinforcement in areas where the political situation is unstable and conducive to military pressure. Its main bases in the Soviet Union are at Leningrad and Riga in the Baltic, Murmansk in the North, at Odessa in the Black Sea, and Vladivostok in the Pacific. During recent years it has had the use of support facilities in Cuba, Guinea, Somalia (though these may now be at risk), South Yemen and, until recently, Alexandria.

Soviet naval aircraft have been operating regularly from Somalia over the Indian Ocean and from Conakry over the South Atlantic, and the indications are that the base in Somalia was oriented towards becoming a large and permanent air and naval facility, subsequent to the Aid Programme and to the Treaty of Friendship which was negotiated in 1974. There are indications too that Angola might well become another forward operating base, although this would be a bonus and back-up to, rather than a replacement for, Conakry. These facilities overseas are a useful, but no longer indispensable, supplement to the 150 support vessels already mentioned.

So far as the pattern of Soviet Fleet deployments is concerned, they have in recent years kept forty-odd surface ships, including auxiliaries, and fifteen submarines, constantly on station in the Mediterranean. Known in NATO as the Sovmedron, it is not without significance that during the Arab–Israeli conflicts and the Lebanese, Cypriot and Libyan crises, this squadron was rapidly and heavily reinforced. Similarly, in the Indian Ocean there has been a Soviet presence of some twenty ships, including auxiliaries, for several years, supplemented by aerial reconnaissance and thus poised astride NATO's lifelines to the Middle and Far East. Apart from these standing maritime forces, ships of the Soviet Navy have been regularly deployed throughout the 1970s in all the oceans—invariably in evidence during NATO exercises, often in considerable strength—and always on or over the horizon when their presence might give support to the political manoeuvring or conflicts which have occurred in the Near East and Africa. The Soviet strategic submarine force is also continually on station, but not in evidence, and not requiring seaborne support or protection.

At this point it may reasonably be asked why the Soviet Union, with no specific task for its surface fleet, and no vital trade or reinforcement routes to protect, should spread such a formidable and costly maritime presence across the oceans. The reason undoubtedly is that in peacetime, success in a worldwide contest for political power is likely, on balance, to go to those who have contrived to build up a dominant military capability, regardless of whether such a capability ever has to be used. And if, for example, the balance of maritime power were allowed to shift so far in favour of the Soviet Union that in a period of tension she could, simply by a show of overwhelming force, isolate Europe by sea and prevent the passage of essential supplies and reinforcements to and from the United States, the effect upon Allied confidence and political cohesion would be profound.

This is a heroic story, not of Phoenix rising from the ashes because there were no ashes to speak of from which to rise. Rather is it an account of a development almost unique in history, possibly of similar importance (though of a quite different nature) to the development and deployment of their nuclear-powered ships and nuclear weapons. It is not too fanciful to suggest that it took about the same length of time and probably cost about the same amount of money. It is not fanciful but fact to observe that it is a parallel example of the remorseless Soviet determination to achieve, if not superiority, then certainly parity. This has not yet been reached at sea, but on any projection of the trend there can be no doubt that it can and, one must suppose, will be reached unless there is a dramatic shift of policy on one side or the other, or both. An attempt will be made in later chapters to assess what effect this has already had, and could have, on the military balance, and what might be done by NATO better to deter any threat which this formidable new engine of war may pose.

CHAPTER VIII

FAMILY AFFAIRS

Accidents and even quarrels happen in the best regulated families. Some members of a family, particularly if it is a large one, are taller, brighter, braver or richer than the others; some are better at making things, and others are better in the world of ideas. But they are all bound together by ties of blood, by a common sense of purpose, by shared experience and shared upbringing, and (although it may be below the surface at times) by affection. There is in short a very strong sense of belonging to the same closely-knit tribe and it is interesting that the Chinese and the Jews probably feel this sense of family more deeply than most other peoples and, which is more to the point, do more about it. It is tempting and not entirely contrived to think of NATO as a family, sharing many of the characteristics and the strengths and weaknesses of families but with the basic tie being not of blood but of shared ideals, and a shared perception of the democratic way of life which they are determined to lead. So we shall take a look at the NATO partnership in family terms, both at the whole family and at some of its members.

NATO quarrels, as has been mentioned earlier, cannot always be decided finally, any more than family ones, by the relatives of those at odds. But a forum for open discussion can be made available, as can collective wisdom and experience and, above all, a very strongly-shared wish to end the quarrel with no loss of face—much less of tangibles—by either of the errant sons. In a more positive and agreeable way the NATO family can, and indeed must, discuss all kinds of matters which directly affect their personal circumstances and can only be handled jointly because they are too difficult or too large to be dealt with singly. This, indeed, is the essence of the Organisation, and how the machine works at all its levels. And by stretching this simile a little further one can almost see and touch the strong sense of unity which has developed over thirty years of weathering together crises large and small, and the mutual satisfaction that comes from having jointly started and continued a great endeavour which has been an unqualified success.

So let us now survey our connections—not with that rather brutal frankness so normal and even irresistible to the participants of the moment in a human family, but more in the detached and objective manner of a very old friend. Such a trusted friend would feel free and be competent to mention what in family terms would be called character differences, and in any terms differences of circumstances. In Alliance terms this would have to include the different constraints and pressures and dominant objectives which arise quite naturally from national history, as do the form and methods individual states have developed for the conduct of both their internal and external affairs.

He would start, because it is so clear a distinction, with the two branches of the family which are separated by the Ocean from which the Organisation takes its name. It is not difficult to enumerate differences of style and method, of resources and capability, of experience and of simple power and influence between the North American partners and those in Europe. If this were attempted (which it will not be here), it would be of the highest importance to keep always in mind, and give equal weight to, the similarity of ideas which binds them together and which has been proved to be much more durable and important than any differences in detail.

Straight away it must be recognised that the United States, having achieved super-power status not only in the Alliance but throughout the non-Communist world, is by far the most powerful of the NATO Allies and that this status arises from and is maintained by wealth, technological excellence, and a vast industrial potential. Also, experience (most unhappy at times) of fighting as the leading Ally in a major limited war in Korea and another war in Vietnam almost but not entirely unaided, has moulded, even if not directly, its policies and approach to NATO problems. Canada, with infinitely less wealth and a smaller though not unimportant technical power-base, has played a part, which other Allies have not, in peace-keeping operations in many parts of the Third World. These two partners comprise the Western pillar of the North Atlantic community and there is little profit in debating whether it is stronger or taller or wider or more important than the European pillar, because unless both bear the weight of the traffic the Atlantic bridge would quickly collapse.

One of the problems about this bridge which is seldom examined as a subject in its own right, but is instinctively recognised by all who have had a part to play in Alliance business, is the sheer difficulty of communication across this vital ocean. It is not a question of language, although this does have some effect, but is much more usually a question of a failure of perception on both sides of the Atlantic about what is actually happening (or even what people wish to happen) on the other. This is as true of ideas as it is of weapons systems or political initiatives, and in a strange way some disarray in the Alliance has frequently arisen through this simple inability to communicate satisfactorily. It is, on the face of it, absurd that this communication gap should exist at all when goodwill and trust and shared intentions are common, and have been so for thirty years. But it does exist and as in so many other relationships we must take life as it is and not as we would like it to be—or even, sometimes, think it is. The solution, as in most other fields of human endeavour, must lie in the taking of great care to avoid misunderstanding, especially of motives. On the credit side of this page in our joint ledger must be entered the fact that despite this continuing difficulty of communication, the links which bind the transatlantic members of the family together have always stood the strain.

Without going right through the thirteen European members of the family, it is possible to pick out several instances where particular national hopes and fears create difficulties of one sort or another in the smooth functioning of the Organisation. Taking first the Federal Republic of Germany, which was the last member to sign the Treaty and which provides by far the greatest land-force contribution to the conventional Allied order of battle, one must remember above all the sensitivity of this great partner to the fact that it is in the very front line and is in a country which has been politically divided. Moreover the industrial heartland is geographically narrow and, apart from the very high concentration of population (which in itself is difficult to deal with in both military and political terms), it is here above all that territory cannot be traded for time. And it is here too that the shock of war would first be felt, and it is here that if a massive attack should be launched with little warning, the brunt would be borne, and it is here above all that theatre nuclear weapons, if used at all, would be most likely to fall. Add to these acutely sensitive facts that it is also here that a million men equipped for Armageddon with every known modern engine of war stand eyeball to eyeball, and that it is here that the Bundeswehr stands shoulder-to-shoulder with the forces of five other Allies, and it is not surprising that German voices should and must be heard loud and clear at the Council table.

Dodging southward to meet a totally different set of problems, one can look both as a whole and at the components separately of the Southern Region. Here we have had, unhappily, a classic demonstration of the effect of family quarrels leading to a manifest weakening of Allied political cohesion, together with some undoubted diminution in military capability. The Southern Region has always posed difficult problems in military terms, if for no other reason than because the separate national territories of Turkey, Greece and Italy—leaving France aside for the moment—are not contiguous and Greece and Turkey each have a common frontier with one or more of the Warsaw Pact countries. In spite of this, the military difficulties are manageable provided the surrounding political and economic factors are normal, but in recent years this has not been so. Italy has passed through a deep economic recession, with the inevitable consequential reduction in the resources she has been able to devote to defence, and this has been compounded by considerable and lengthy political instability. Nevertheless Italian forces, although considerably reduced in number, are now being vigorously re-equipped, political stability has been enhanced, and economic recovery is under way.

Regrettably, the quarrel between Greece and Turkey over the events in Cyprus in 1974 and others since have not been settled. The inherent difficulties to which this has led from the point of view of the Alliance have been seriously complicated by an interruption in the previously smooth bilateral relations between each of these countries and the United States. In the midst of their disagreement over Cyprus, the Greek and Turkish Governments share a common difficulty brought about by the failure by the United States to renew its separate Defence Co-operation Agreements (DCAs) with each of them. For although both Greece and Turkey spend a higher proportion of their national income on defence than any other Ally, and while each country has numerically very large forces (Turkey, for example, has the largest army in the Alliance), their lack of economic development means that the actual sums nationally available for defence are insufficient adequately to equip and maintain their forces. Thus the DCAs are of an overriding importance to the maintenance of each country's contribution to the Alliance and hence to the military cohesion of the integrated forces at the disposal of the Commander in Chief Southern Region. So while there is nothing inherently unsound about this vital Region (except perhaps the Command structure which can be discussed elsewhere), the straightforward military effectiveness in the south-east extremity of the Alliance must realistically be regarded as a good deal less than satisfactory until these outstanding, interlocking, complicated and very difficult political problems are solved. This difficulty is compounded by the fact that the major bones of contention lie outside the NATO umbrella.

To return briefly to France, as a member of the Alliance intimately involved in the affairs of both the Southern and Central Regions, both as the Western cornerstone of the Alliance in Europe and as an individual, it has already been remarked that the withdrawal of the French forces from the integrated military structure of the Alliance (although the complicated mechanics of it were brilliantly handled on both sides at the time) has undoubtedly diminished the total effectiveness of SACEUR's command. Without trying to

examine the political possibilities which lie ahead, tempting
and fascinating though this would be, there are certain things
which can be said about the situation which has resulted from
the French withdrawal. Possibly the first is that French
Governments, through the mouths of successive Presidents,
Prime Ministers, Foreign Ministers and Defence Ministers, are
on the public record as having said that, notwithstanding the
events of 1966, France is still a full member of the Alliance and
in particular still subscribes to Article 5 of the Treaty. This of
course is excellent news, although the interpretation of it both
within the Alliance and by the Warsaw Pact could give rise to
potentially dangerous misunderstandings.

But neither the Allies nor outsiders should forget that France
is among the fairly small group of first-rate powers behind the
two super-powers, and specifically that France is a nuclear
power. By immense determination, with no external assistance,
and by the expenditure of enormous resources of men, money
and material, France now disposes of strategic and theatre
nuclear weapons. This has very important and far-reaching
political as well as military effects, not only on her position
within the Alliance but within the total balance of power. It is
neither appropriate nor necessary here to discuss whether
France was right or not so to dispose of her resources as to
acquire this status, but the unarguable fact is that she has done
so. It is possible to discuss at length and speculate in principle
and in detail on the effect of this third nuclear power within
NATO upon a host of interconnected subjects, but what
cannot be denied is that as a result there exists a third decision
centre, within NATO, for the use of these ultimate weapons.
And any would-be aggressor must take very close and careful
account of it. In the same way, in the conventional or—as the
French prefer to call it—the classical balance, French forces
are very much to be reckoned with. Although, quite naturally,
these are now less well equipped than they would have been
had not so many resources been allocated to France's nuclear
arsenal, her army, navy and air force are by European
standards numerous, well-equipped, well-trained, well-
motivated and well-led. Agreements exist, mostly at the level
of the major Commanders, for co-operation between these

forces and those of the Alliance, sometimes on a bilateral or trilateral basis, sometimes on an Alliance-wide basis, and this is wholly good. A visible demonstration of this lies in the frequent joint exercises which take place in which French forces take part alongside those of one or more NATO partners. An equally clear demonstration of the continuing political interest of France in the NATO military equation was given in 1975, when, following the announcement by the United Kingdom that her resident maritime forces would be withdrawn from the Mediterranean, a substantial part of the French fleet was transferred there from the Atlantic. This more or less coincided with the fall-out from the Cyprus troubles the previous summer, and demonstrated with customary French neatness a realistic appreciation of the realities of life, the danger of a power vacuum in this—to France—vital sea, and the mutual feedback of a simultaneous political and military initiative. It should also allow any with doubts about it to feel re-assured that NATO's French connection really is still one of the family.

In this loose and discursive tour of the attitudes and attributes of some members of the NATO family, it would seem a feeble omission for me not at least to refer to Britain's contribution, and the way it has been and is regarded both at home and by her Allies. First let it be said at once that the Royal Navy is the third largest in the world, the most modern, probably the best equipped and at least as well if not better trained than any navy afloat. This is not at all surprising for an island nation whose ships have been undefeated in a war since anyone can remember, but it is a very major contribution to Alliance solidarity, capability and security, which is often insufficiently recognised by Britain's European partners, although it almost certainly is so recognised by any would-be aggressor. It should be understood that this reference to the Royal Navy embraces, as it has for many years now, the maritime forces of the Royal Air Force, and it is proper and normal in assessing capability today to think in terms of maritime forces comprising those who fly over it as well as those on and under the sea. The British Army of the Rhine is the largest, best equipped, best trained and best led of the armies in Northern Army Group, and is readily recognised to be so not only by the Commander in Chief Central Region and his Supreme Commander, but by the other four countries that contribute to this Army Group. Nevertheless its effectiveness and hence its deterrent power undoubtedly suffer from the need almost to double its numbers to be battle-ready, and from the logistic problems imposed by lengthy lines of communication, lack of common and even interoperable—much less standardised—equipment. These are important shortcomings, although not by any means entirely of the making of the United Kingdom. Royal Air Force Germany is, like Rhine Army, the largest, best equipped and most effective component of the Second Allied Tactical Air Force and recognised as such by its Allies and Superior Commanders, although it also suffers to much the same extent from some of the limitations of the land forces just mentioned. This, however, is not by any means the whole contribution of the Royal Air Force to the Alliance, particularly bearing in mind the creation in 1976 of the new NATO major subordinate command of United Kingdom Air directly subordinate to SACEUR. This command, with responsibilities also to SACLANT, has the immensely important task not only of direct support to these two Supreme Commands and to the defence of the United Kingdom Air Defence Region, but also for the provision and readiness and defence of the bases and transit facilities for massive augmentation and reinforcement forces from the United States Air Force normally based in North America but earmarked for the European theatre. This is all good and heartening news for Britain and the Alliance. It is also good and heartening news that British expertise in all NATO's political and military and politico-military fields of endeavour is still very highly regarded, to the extent that at all the integrated Headquarters the sheer professional competence of British officers and officials alike is second to none, and recognised to be so.

Thus British advice and British appreciations of developing situations are given much more weight than her simple quantitative contribution would otherwise merit, and long may this continue. What is not good news is the way in which successive reductions in the British contribution to the total

Allied effort have been made in recent years. The reductions
in themselves have been important, and made too frequently
for the comfort of our Allies. Much has been said and done and
written on this subject; suffice it to say that through the
mouths of the Secretary General and successive Chairmen of
the Military Committee, NATO's distress and regret at these
successive reductions have been made luminously clear. One
of our distinguished Supreme Commanders summed up a
generally shared Allied reaction to them in graphic terms when
he commented: 'It is like being nibbled to death by ducks—
none of the bites hurts much by itself but the cumulative effect
could be terminal.'

A less quantifiable but almost certainly equally important
feature of this reduction process has been psychological.
Britain has been immensely well regarded within the Alliance
ever since she played a major part in its formation, and this
regard flows not just from the unique burden she bore when
facing a world in arms alone in 1940, and the subsequent
victory, but from centuries of history before the comparatively
brief span since the Treaty was signed. It is distressing to
Britain's friends and allies that their confidence in this hitherto
robust bastion of freedom, and the epitome of all that has been
best in the conduct of Alliance affairs, should have been
reduced to the point where no Ally can now be certain what
Britain's contribution will be next year or in three years' time.
It is remembered and appreciated by the other members of the
family that for many years the United Kingdom's Defence
White Paper has pledged (in its first or another early para-
graph) that NATO is the linchpin of Britain's defence policy,
and it is equally recognised that very serious economic
difficulties have made it virtually impossible to maintain the
British contribution at the proportionate level of the founding
years, but an unequivocal assurance that support at the
present or a higher level can be expected to continue is what is
so desperately needed from the point of view of the Commanders
who have to plan, the Military Committee which has to give
the Commanders their policy guidance, and the North Atlantic
Council itself which is responsible for the whole governance of
the Alliance. If it is true that mutual confidence is the only vital

element of cohesion, then it must be said that this has been weakened by these successive British reductions, and this demands urgent attention.

The last of the founding fathers of the family to be mentioned here is Portugal, partly because her role and participation have been markedly different from those of her fellow-signatories, and also because she has given her Allies (and herself too come to that) some anxious moments. For much of the first twenty-five years Portugal spent proportionately more on Defence than any other member, but nearly all the resources thus made available were deployed outside Europe and either not at all, or extremely indirectly, in support of NATO. It is certainly, and happily, true that this important part of the Iberian peninsula was always available to the Major NATO Commanders principally for maritime defence, and that the Portuguese naval and air forces played as full a part as their numbers, equipment and state of training permitted, but the consequent addition to our order of battle in those days must, realistically, be assessed as small. Nevertheless, since the very welcome outcome of the dramatic events of 1974, and the consequent return to a democratic form of government, it is possible to look forward to a marked improvement in our posture, not only in Portugal itself but in her islands too. This is good news for both SACLANT and SACEUR, under whose imaginative initiatives Portugese land, sea and air forces are being re-structured, re-equipped and re-trained for specific and useful NATO roles. This brief mention would be incomplete without reference to the fact that there were at one time, albeit briefly, Communist ministers in the Portuguese Government. This event, which has direct relevance to the possibility of the same thing occurring in other Allied countries, was handled at both the political and military level in a commendably calm and reasonable manner thanks to a shared desire to solve the problem in other capitals, at Evere and in Lisbon. It provides, in passing, the best grounds for the hope expressed in a later chapter that a pragmatic approach to so emotive a subject is likely to be more successful than one based on a pre-conceived 'hard-line' doctrine.

Finally we must look at a country which is not a member

of the family but, to stretch the analogy nearly to breaking-point, might perhaps become so by marriage. This convoluted reference is of course made to Spain, and as with most of the family affairs already discussed, much has already been written and said about the possibility of Spain joining the Alliance. There can be no reasonable doubt that NATO would be stronger were Spain to join it. A glance at the map, particularly focussed on the Southern Region, the Mediterranean and its exit to the Atlantic, is sufficient to show without lengthy discussion that the defence of sea and air communications, of the Mediterranean in particular and the Southern Region as a whole, would be immensely simplified and more effective were our lines of defence continuous rather than interrupted as they now are at the south-western corner. It is true that the simple addition of Spain to the Fifteen would not at once greatly augment NATO's order of battle, because for many years the Spanish armed forces have been structured and equipped for a totally different role. Nevertheless the contribution that would be made in terms of facilities based upon geography (rather like that made by Iceland) would be of immense value by itself, and with careful planning but without enormous expenditure, well-equipped modern forces, particularly for reinforcement, could quite quickly be created for the land, sea and air elements of NATO's integrated military structure.

These factors seem to be straightforward and indisputable, but the political implications of an application, or on the other hand an invitation, to join are immensely complicated, and certain to reach out into areas which are almost wholly non-military, like the Council of Europe, the EEC and similar organisations of an economic or political nature. Moreover if such a marriage were to be contemplated, then, as is customary in Western countries in this day and age, both parties would have to be willing. Neither NATO nor the Spanish Government has said formally that it wishes so to enlarge the Alliance, and it is as large and complex a problem for the Spanish Government as for the Alliance itself to weigh up the advantages and disadvantages for them of doing so. It seems possible to observe, however, that having successfully restored a democratic form of government under a constitutional monarchy, it would be entirely normal for Spain to wish now to be treated like other Western European states, and be able to join this as well as other institutions to which most Western European states belong. It seems sensible for any approach by either side to be made in this spirit and it is to be hoped that if it is, it will be received in like manner.

It will be noted that several members of the family have been left out of this look around it. This is not, of course, because they are more or less good or naughty, more or less rich or important, or for any reason other than that it appears that the pressing problems for the Alliance today can be found in the members who have been discussed. Not every problem, but most of them.

CHAPTER IX

THE HIGHER DIRECTION OF NATO

Chapter I traced very briefly the evolution of the highest levels of the political and military sides of the NATO house during their first twenty-five years. It is desirable to look rather more closely at the North Atlantic Council and the North Atlantic Military Committee (to give them their full official titles), and to look some way down their family trees, if the manner and method of dealing with some of their day-to-day work and the current and future problems this work throws up are to be at all easily visualised. This is often done by printing and then referring to diagrams of the 'family trees' (interestingly described in American as 'wiring diagrams' and in NATO-ese as 'organigrams'), but such diagrams, if complete, are very busy and difficult to read, and if incomplete lead to charges of favouritism. In any event they involve too much detail and blur the important lines of consultation, control, decision and command with which this chapter is more directly concerned.

In essence the organisation for the higher direction of Alliance affairs is similar to that of a national government, with a 'Cabinet' (the Council) and various Cabinet committees dealing with Defence, External Affairs, Money, Construction, Communications, Forward Planning and so on. In an extension of this similarity, we find the 'Chiefs of Staff Committee' (the Military Committee) with its own web of specialist committees for Plans, Logistics, Communications, Standardisation, and so on and their Commanders in Chief in the field represented by the Headquarters of the Major NATO Commanders and their many Allied subordinates. To complete the analogy we find at Evere the customary common services of Financial Control, Personnel, Public Relations, Science and those other essential elements of governmental support which are also found in capitals.

There are some general observations on the NATO machine which should be made before attempting to look at a few of the details, of which nearly all will be seen to be constraints on the smooth and effective functioning of the system, and especially of its international members, while others are shared by national governments, and yet others are peculiar (possibly in both senses of the word) to NATO. The most obvious and also the most important difference to which reference has already been made—and will be made again—is that NATO has no mandatory powers and its decisions must be unanimous. The difficulty of reaching such decisions, which has also been mentioned before, stems from the membership of the Council and Military Committee being drawn from so many sovereign and democratic states. This is even exaggerated, although it should not be, in the Military Committee where there are not only the national pressures to be massaged into unanimity but the not always identical hopes and fears of three Services to be moulded into one coherent policy in capitals before exposure to the multinational gaze in Evere. And this gives rise to the paradox, which even some quite experienced NATO-watchers seem regularly to miss, that the international officials and officers who have thrown away their national hats to produce the best Alliance solutions report to multinational bodies in the Council and Military Committee whose members, speaking on national instructions from their capitals, too frequently frustrate these loyal international solutions. So it must always be borne in mind when considering the governance of NATO, or any other aspect of Alliance business in which 'NATO' is used as an umbrella term, where the actual power of decision lies. Evere proposes, but the sad truth is that in practice, capitals always dispose. The final constraint to be mentioned at this stage is that NATO has no money of its own. It has the use of what might be described as a variable annuity, subscribed, usually without much enthusiasm, by its members for certain very explicitly defined purposes under the most carefully scrutinised control.

The Council, to come to the particular, has been described as a 'diplomatic workshop' and also as a 'standing committe of [member] governments' and it merits both descriptions. The

Permanent Representatives are the personal representatives of all departments of their Government and are thus truly plenipotentiary. It may be said that all Ambassadors are so described, and this is usually but not always true, but it is of the highest importance to the Alliance that those at Evere really are so, since they are required to conduct at the highest level day-to-day business which covers the whole spectrum of international affairs. In times of tension or crisis, the success or failure of the whole NATO enterprise can well depend on the speed and the authority with which these Ambassadors conduct our corporate business. It is a great comfort to one who has sat at their table for three years and watched them for another three, to record that the Alliance is well served by extremely able, experienced and decisive diplomatists who are more than a match in all respects for any likely opposition. Their function, though it is seldom stated and is often over-looked, is to transmit and receive and re-transmit, so that their Governments may not only make their own views known but be quickly and expertly informed of the views of their Allies. This is a highly skilled business.

The Council meets at least once a week in Permanent Session and it is significant that the first item on the agenda is invariably 'Political Subjects', and under this handy umbrella virtually any matter of topical importance can be dealt with early, rather than being shuffled—as it so often is elsewhere—into a rag-bag of 'any other business' at the end of the meeting when all hands are tired and want their lunch. This item is normally taken in a restricted attendance session and no record of it is issued, so that discussion can be as free and uninhibited as possible. The frequent and routine nature of this meeting ensures that all members are in a truly 'permanent session', and it is of interest that to conduct the same business bilaterally would require one hundred separate meetings (which would quite certainly not produce nearly such a good answer). All subjects of common interest can be discussed and sooner or later are, the only taboo being those matters which concern the internal affairs of any of the members. This is, if there were no other reason (and there are plenty) why NATO is not, and can never be, an organisation for settling disagreements between its members, as has been said as bluntly as possible in the first chapter.

The Defence Planning Committee, which is composed of the same people but fewer of them (France and Greece do not take part for reasons already explained) meets on a similar routine basis to the Council, and has for all practical purposes the same authority, in the special field of Defence. It is probably surprising to learn that over any year this Committee meets much less frequently than does the Council, and some reasons for this and some of its effects will be examined in more detail in a later chapter. At this, the highest, NATO level we are concerned with only two more bodies, the Nuclear Defence Affairs Committee and the Nuclear Planning Group whose composition has already been mentioned. These two also meet at Ambassadorial level, regularly but not so frequently, and at Defence Ministers level twice a year.

Below these 'Cabinet'-type consultations, day-to-day business of all kinds is carried on by an intricate web of committees, working groups, panels and agencies, some informal and some formal, some standing and some *ad hoc*, some international, some national, some hybrid, some meeting at Evere and some in capitals, amounting at the most recent count to more than 300. That great Defence Minister Herr Leber, and most of his colleagues, have said quite loudly that this is far too many, and no one who has worked at Evere would disagree, more particularly those at the level of 'Indians' (as opposed to 'Chiefs' in these sensitive days) who spend so much time at meetings within this network that they hardly ever see their desks, at least not in daylight. It may be noted parenthetically that this is why any complete 'wiring diagram' of them would be busy to the point of frenzy. It is, unfortunately, easier to say this than it is to reduce them, and they do not exceed *pro rata* the proliferation that is evident in most capitals; furthermore, it is almost certainly in the nature of a fifteen-nation 'government' that the soft option of setting up an '*ad hoc* (*et al.*) group' to deal with awkward matters that do not obviously belong in the main stream is more than usually prevalent. At all events there they are, and while their incestuous breeding has now largely been controlled, they are not likely to decrease very much unless, or until, some really tough hatchet man with nothing else to do is hired to cut them down.

Turning to the Military side of the NATO house, it is necessary first to establish whether one is stepping down, moving sideways or moving (slightly) upwards. Status and its symbols, like the poor in times gone by, are always with us in the brave new world of Organisation Man, and in this NATO is no exception. Some of the military, whether in capitals or international headquarters, have been trained (instructed?) to refer always to their 'political masters'; others, perhaps more bolshie by nature, tend to insert another word before 'masters' and there is a third group, on the whole more sensible and certainly more tactful, who, if they have to refer to them at all, use the euphemism which of course is used in this book, namely 'political partners'. However deeply the proponents of any of these three formulations may feel, the facts of life are quite plain and, what is unusual, they are written down just as plainly. The Council is the supreme political instrument for making, implementing and projecting Alliance policies, and the Military Committee is the highest military authority for advising upon before, and executing after, Council decisions are taken. The Chairman of the Military Committee is charged with the dual function of representing the collective view of the Allied military at Chiefs of Staff (Defence) level and being, in his person, the principal military adviser to the Council. Argumentation will doubtless continue around this, on the whole, virtuous circle for as long as NATO is necessary, but enjoyable or exasperating as it may be depending on the point of view, it is not in practice important; on any reading of the Treaty and of the Ottawa Declaration, NATO is more than a military Alliance. The fact that it depends for its survival on military power does not make the military element in it overridingly important, though it is more important than the political imperative which gave it birth and still cements it together, simply to the extent that without a successful military deterrent the other activities of the Allies would have no viable point of departure.

In this (only moderately humble) spirit it is of considerable general importance to look, and to look quite critically, at the

Command Structure as it stands today and to speculate, as will be done in a later chapter, whether it is a suitable candidate for alteration. In the same way as the political side of the house has been treated from the top down, we can best start with the Military Committee and the Major NATO Commanders. Their responsibilities and duties and the inter-relationship between those two are very clearly defined in NATO documents on which Council—and thus Allied Governmental— holy water has been duly sprinkled. The actual discharge of these duties is, either in spite of or because of these documents, potentially awkward, and it is necessary to glance back over our fairly short history to discern from where this awkwardness arises in order to have a sound basis for an understanding of the *status quo*, and to discuss—as will be done later—some ways of devising a more responsive yet equally effective system.

At the beginning, we saw that the military affairs of the infant Alliance which were then, notwithstanding the language of the Treaty, unquestionably dominant, were entrusted to a Standing Group consisting of France, the United Kingdom and the United States in Washington, with the addition a year later of the Supreme Allied Commander (in) Europe, who was located in France. No great exercise of imagination is needed to appreciate that, until this structure was fundamentally changed sixteen years later, SACEUR became in both political and military eyes in Europe 'Mr. Military NATO'; this was especially true of the continental European Allies who for historical, and to some extent emotional, reasons were and still largely are land animals. It became normal—and it was natural, respectable and not surprising that this should be so— for the Council to refer (and defer) to the most important military figure who was on the spot, more particularly because he was also the personal embodiment of the United States' commitment to the Alliance, and upon whose nuclear power almost total reliance for deterrence was then placed. Despite the actual authority of the Standing Group, it was 3,000 miles away, and communication with it—in the sense of a meeting of minds as well as the mechanical process—was a good deal less than instant. So despite the creation of the other two essentially maritime major NATO commands of the

Atlantic and Channel, and the steady development of something approaching today's Military Committee, the focus of military advice and power remained, for many years after the reorganisation which followed the French withdrawal from the integrated military structure, in the headquarters and person of SACEUR. Even today there are those who, while recognising the pre-eminent position of the Military Committee and its Chairman, and the equivalent status of SACLANT and to an admittedly smaller extent the Commander in Chief Channel (CINCHAN), still have a gut feeling that SACEUR is really their man. All this, although intangible, does not help the orderly discharge of Alliance military business and, it must be said, leads to some abrasiveness between Evere and Mons on the one hand and Mons and Norfolk (Virginia) and Northwood (Middlesex) on the other. With pleasure one can say that this certainly does not apply today in the castles or flagships of the Generals and Admirals concerned, but it must equally be recorded that, at perhaps 'red' Colonel level, it still lurks not far below the surface. Time and commonsense, rather than reorganisation, will cure this not very important malaise.

With that somewhat lengthy but necessary background, it is possible to look at the skeleton of the military body and describe rather briefly how it works. At NATO Headquarters in Evere, the Military Committee and its immediate support are organised in very much the same way as the Council. The Chairman, whose authority and function is, in his own sphere, closely similar to that of the Secretary General and to whom several references have already been made, is elected by the Chiefs of Defence customarily for a term of two years, normally extended to three. It may be observed here that this is not long enough (unless of course the Chiefs select a dud) and three to four or even five would be much better. The Chairman has a Deputy who is always a United States officer, at three-star level, normally rotating between the three services; apart from his customary Deputy's responsibilities, he is responsible for the co-ordination of the military input to all nuclear matters and to Mutual and Balanced Force Reduction work, through the International Military Staff. The Deputy does not take the

Chair at meetings in Chiefs of Defence Session, so that should the Chairman be absent this duty would devolve upon the Honorary President. At this top level of international officers, these two are joined by the Director of the International Military Staff who is a three-star officer of any service and nation, also elected by the Military Committee, and customarily serving for two to three years. The Military Committee is charged by the Council with the peacetime task of 'recommending [all] those measures considered necessary for the common defence of the NATO area' (read a second time, more slowly, this is a wide remit by any standards). As NATO's highest military authority, the Committee is the body to which the Supreme Allied Commanders Europe and Atlantic and the Commander in Chief Channel (and the Canada/US Regional Planning Group for good measure) are responsible; to all of these it will give guidance on policy. In addition, fourteen NATO military agencies serve directly under the authority of the Military Committee, among which must be mentioned the Military Agency for Standardisation in Evere, the Advisory Group for Aerospace Research and Development in Paris, and the NATO Defence College in Rome, as well as several communication agencies.

The Military Committee meets in Permanent Session once a week at least, and at Chiefs of Defence level always three and sometimes four times a year. The Agenda normally opens with a worldwide intelligence briefing which covers important events outside as well as within the NATO area, and this is followed usually by another briefing on a specialised topic of current interest quite often given by a visiting team from a capital or Military Headquarters. Of course, the Military Committee, unlike the Council, has no equivalent of the Defence Planning Committee, because the members are drawn only from those countries contributing forces to the integrated military structure (Iceland, which contributes facilities but not forces, is entitled to send a civilian but never does). They have, however, a device which makes the conduct of their business very close to that of Council/DPC practice (and in certain respects neater) by forming their agenda into Parts I and II in such a way that the Chief of the French Military Mission (to the Military Committee) attends Part I but withdraws for the items in Part II. This is possibly less divisive and certainly enables the Chairman to take a commonsense view of the inevitable 'grey area' matters, which could in principle require or not require French attendance. It remains only to say that the members of the Military Committee in Permanent Session are Flag and General officers of considerable seniority and wide experience who have been found to be both wise and morally brave in their united determination to reach agreement or a strong consensus view on all their problems for onward transmission, either on paper or by the mouth of their Chairman, to their political partners—who take the decisions—in the Council or Defence Planning Committee or both.

Three other features, at least, of the 'Milreps' (as the NATO acronym has it) are worth a mention. They represent their Chief of Defence, but not their Ministry or their Government, and the extent to which their views coincide with those of their Ambassador (NATO-ese 'Perm Rep') depends on the interface between Government Departments in the capitals more than it does on relations between their two top men at Evere. Some Milreps are in fact attached by their Governments loosely to their Perm Reps as advisers, or more closely as actual members of their Delegation (this latter solution is happily rare because it is almost guaranteed not to work). Lastly the Military Committee has a very strong corporate sense of family and its members make perhaps still more strenuous efforts to bind themselves together than even the Council members do. This is good news, normally, for their Chairman but becomes less so if they get the bit between their teeth and bolt down a side road. This, however, does not often happen because the Chairman is normally a more experienced practitioner and ensures that the side road is blocked before his team has decided to bolt.

Operational Command, under the three Major NATO Commanders, is organised on a geographically regional basis with the customary levels of command typically under, in each Region, a Commander (known as a Major Subordinate Commander) at four-star level, with Army Group and Tactical Air Force Commanders at three- (sometimes four-) star level below him and known as Principal Subordinate Commanders; and so on down the scale through the Corps, Division, Brigade, and Unit levels to the actual man with the musket. This is standard practice, and is only recorded to draw attention to the two facts that the Commanders down to Principal Subordinate Commander level are NATO Commanders, and below that level are national commanders commanding national units or formations, and that while this organisation exists and goes about its daily business in peacetime, only the various Head-quarters are permanently activated. The sharp-end forces and their support elements do not come under command until pre-viously agreed phases of the NATO Alert System have been passed through. There is a great deal more which could be said about this, but it is highly specialised and, in the author's view, out of place here, although a further glance will be directed at it in a later chapter where some possible improvements to the Command Structure will be discussed.

There are two further extremely important features of the international civil and military staffs which must be included in this description of the superstructure. These staffs have been co-located for only ten years and their interface is consequently neither as smooth nor as mutually confident as it is in capitals where, sometimes, they have been co-located for centuries. This is getting better all the time, but there remain traces of the 'we and they' syndrome which can only be removed by the passage of events and years. Finally there is money, and while in NATO circles it is not 'the root of all evil' (or even has much evil about it) it is at the very heart of our affairs. Having said earlier that NATO has no money of its own, it nevertheless has the spending of quite large sums on commonly-funded projects. To put this into perspective, the yearly total is about 180 million international units of account (IAU) which, at the end-1977 rate of exchange, is equivalent to about £360 million. The biggest share, more than half, is spent on 'infrastructure' for the construction of facilities, one-third on the Military Headquarters (of which there are about forty) and the tiny sum of 15 million IAU, or less than one-tenth of the total on the Civil Budget, which of course includes the actual Head-quarters of the Alliance at Evere.

This brings in its train the normal apparatus of civil and military budget committees, financial controllers and auditors, all internationally manned but kept under an extremely beady eye by similarly qualified experts from capitals united in their determination to account for every last pfennig. Suffice it to say that except possibly for an accountant and the Controllers who actually do it, this work is not the most riveting part of the 'higher direction'. But it must be recorded that all financial matters concerning so-called NATO expenditure fall under the corporate responsibility of the Council.

Thus is the Higher Direction of NATO organised and thus does it function. It obviously could not do so without the underpinning of staff at all levels from senior officials, including scientists, down to messengers and cleaners and—perhaps often forgotten in capitals—the essential and numerous staff of interpreters and translators without which this international and multinational (not the same thing) headquarters could not work at all. One may note, only in passing, that the numbers of staff compare favourably with those in capitals, and its international members are less numerous than those with whom they work in the national delegations. It should be added that the international staffs are better paid than they would be in their own country, but less well paid (despite heroic efforts by the Secretary General) than in other major international headquarters—for example, the EEC in the same city.

CHAPTER X

NATO STRATEGY

Strategy is a big word which means very different things depending on its context. It is now normal to have a 'strategy' for reducing unemployment, for controlling pollution, for selling things, for growing more food or for controlling the growth of population. The word used to mean military strategy, which over the centuries has been as readily explained as it has been understood, the results being a clear indicator of success or failure. In modern usage, it rather pretentiously implies the (unusual) possession by the strategist of some mystique and special skill or intellectual perception, amounting in the minds of some practitioners almost to the status of divine revelation, although most often it means no more than that there is a 'plan' for dealing with the subject under treatment. This, in fact, is just about what it means in the context of NATO. The 'subject under treatment' by NATO is very much larger and more complex than any of the examples just given, seeing that it is the North Atlantic Treaty and its later refinement in the Ottawa Declaration. So it may not be too pretentious to refer to 'NATO Strategy', as long as it is understood that its implementation is not in the exclusive hands of statesmen and generals working in an intellectual stratosphere, but that it is the very life-work of countless men and women in several disciplines and at all levels in fifteen capitals, Alliance Headquarters and a host of supporting agencies spread throughout the length and breadth of NATO.

Strategy is defined in handbooks used at staff colleges and in other places devoted to its study, many of them indeed incorporating the word in their title. These definitions vary, but stripped of frills all of them normally amount to saying that strategy is the business of defining as precisely as possible *what* you are setting out to do and then working out *how* you intend to do it. This may seem a rather earthy description to some of the professionals and most of the amateurs engaged in this class of work, and unlikely to attract funds from rich trusts or lead to many doctorates, but it is none the less true for that.

So far as NATO is concerned the first part of this task, as has already been said, was the formulation of the Treaty, which cannot be faulted for clarity, lack of ambiguity or completeness. To leave aside for the moment (and only for the pursuit of the hard core of the *how* to do this *what*) the more purely economic and humanitarian aims of the Allies, it can be briefly stated that the essence of NATO strategy is the prevention of aggression occurring against the sovereignty or security of all or even one of its members. The secondary purpose, should deterrence fail and aggression occur whether by miscalculation or design, is to defend and if necessary restore the territorial integrity, security and sovereignty of whichever member may have been attacked. It is this *what* that NATO is formed to achieve. Before discussing the *how*, or the means to implement this strategy, some constraints must be examined.

This involves reverting to what the staff handbooks call the 'factors affecting the aim', or in plainer language what you are up against, what you need to do the job, what you are actually provided with to do it (regrettably not at all the same thing), and what are your options. A good deal of this ground has been covered here already, in discussing the nature of the threat, what deterrence is all about, and the balance of conventional and nuclear forces. However, some more detailed discussion of other aspects is desirable, to complete the frame of the NATO picture.

Because the North Atlantic Treaty is a political document, albeit in the first instance about military matters, it must be said at once that in the implementation of NATO strategy there are practically no matters which are purely political (though they are, one hopes, politically pure), any more than there are more than a few which are purely military. In this endeavour political and military activities must be totally interdependent, indeed indivisible, which is why any lack of cohesion on either side of the house is recognised as the recipe for disaster on both. It is, in general, easier for opponents of NATO, whether outside or inside the family, to drive political wedges between members and so weaken or diminish this essential cohesion, than it is to devise—much less insert or hammer home—military wedges. One does not have to delve deeply into the political history of NATO during thirty years to find frequent examples of (to change the metaphor) political sapping and mining. That nothing of this kind has succeeded is a tribute to the solidarity and deep sense of shared purpose of the Allies, but it also reminds us, if we need to be reminded, of the necessity for perpetual vigilance to spot in good time the attempts which will certainly be made in the future.

The bones of NATO's strategic objective have just been set out, and in the first chapter it was briefly noted how the means of meeting this objective, dictated by the perceived threat and technological progress, changed from the early trip-wire and massive (nuclear) retaliation to any form or degree of armed attack, to the current doctrine of deterrence, forward defence, flexible response and détente. It may be worth repeating in different words that the achievement of this aim in effect requires NATO to possess and be seen to possess the means and the will to confront any threatened or actual aggression, from political pressure or harassment through minor operations and up the escalatory ladder to general (nuclear) war. Success will be achieved, as it has been in the past, if no potential aggressor is led to suppose that his objective could be gained by either the threat or the use of force against any member-nation in the Alliance. It is obvious that within this framework there are many options open to a would-be aggressor which postulate an advantage, and some of these have been mentioned, but there are other less obvious ones such as those which Churchill described as 'picking the fruits of war without the cost of war', of which political or economic threats and wars by proxy are simple examples. These options greatly complicate the task of political and military planners alike when seeking the optimum *how* to achieve the aim.

The blunt instruments available in the military sphere are the elements of conventional forces, theatre nuclear forces and strategic nuclear forces making up the triad of NATO's military power. These have been described already in some detail, and it has been shown that they can be shaped and can be discussed separately, but it is the intricate linkage between them which gives reality to the notion of NATO strategy.

It is necessary to say again that under the flexible response imperative (nothing else makes any sense in the circumstances of today), the conventional forces are the basic and literally vital first element and must never be regarded as what has regrettably often been described as a 'symbolic presence'. The aspect of these classical armies, navies and air forces which poses a real problem for the Alliance is that of deciding upon their size and shape, not only in absolute terms but in relation to one another. There are, for example, three broad options which could be considered, of which the most obvious is the provision of a full conventional capability on land, on the sea and in the air NATO-wide, sufficiently numerous and well equipped in every respect, including support, to be quite certainly capable of dealing with the maximum weight of conventional forces which could be assembled and concentrated against ours. Or we could settle for an intermediate capability which could deal with small-scale attacks anywhere and more than one at a time, or with larger attacks for a limited time with reinforcements and the assured means of getting them wherever they are needed for this time to be extended, or with larger attacks that fail to do as well as either we or an aggressor might expect. At the top (or bottom depending on your point of view) of this scale is a low capability, adequate to deal with small-scale attacks, probes or adventures and to identify major incursions. The first of these is a low-risk high-cost option which nations have made entirely clear goes well beyond what they are prepared to spend. The last—essentially the trip-wire notion—is a high-risk, low- (conventional) cost option which was finally rejected ten years ago, and does not go any way towards meeting the requirements of the flexible response which, as we have seen, is an essential plank in NATO's platform.

Faced with these three possibilities, and there really are no others, NATO has exercised the option of the intermediate capability. This choice, and in all the circumstances it was less of a choice than Hobson's, has some important benefits apart from the evident one of enabling the Allied response to military pressure to be graduated according to the nature of the pressure, and thus be flexible. It ensures also another of the planks of our platform, that of forward defence and this not only makes good military sense but assures those members who are closest to our Eastern boundaries that all their friends are with them to share what hazards may impend. So the visible presence of conventional forces of half-a-dozen member nations in the forward areas not only demonstrates our military capability and determination to fight if deterrence fails, but is a major component of the political and military cohesion from which mutual confidence flows. It is indeed an essential ingredient of that deterrence which is more than a plank in our platform, but is the very keystone of our strategy. It must be observed, in this connection, that should the Allies fail, through lack of will or for any other reason, to provide adequate conventional forces for their chosen strategy, then the only course left will be a return to the trip-wire, high-risk option and to accept the inevitable and highly undesirable consequences. As was remarked in an earlier chapter there are people, some of them highly distinguished, who fear that we are approaching this dire situation already, if we have not actually reached it. This does not affect the strategy, or the explanation of why it was chosen, but it does affect very directly how the strategy should be implemented. It also makes clear beyond any reasonable doubt that this leads directly back to political will and forward to resource allocation, the latter of which is high on the list of NATO's current problems which will be discussed in a separate chapter.

Before leaving the general topic of NATO's strategy it must be said that there are also those, and among them people who are well-informed about these matters, who sincerely believe that NATO strategy as it now stands must be changed, because the circumstances in which it was devised more than ten years ago have so greatly altered. They naturally include, though somewhat on their fringe, those who hold that the Alliance, through failure to provide adequate conventional forces, has already *de facto* been driven back to the trip-wire. It cannot be denied that many of the relevant circumstances are sub-stantially different today from those apparent in 1966, nor can it be said that the exercise of carefully considering our strategy in the light of those differences, is other than a respectable and even a prudent activity. It seems nonetheless that the high-cost low-risk option, while remaining as desirable as it always has been, stands absolutely no chance of being funded unless there is some dramatic change in our perceptions of the threat we have to deter. Nor, rightly or wrongly, would it be an attractive change of political course for Western governments to embark on what would have to be a massive programme of greatly increased conventional forces, when they are (as NATO is) formally pledged to pursue détente. The disadvantages of a return to the high-risk, low-cost option of the trip-wire have already been mentioned, and would indeed be so grave in military, political and psychological terms as almost certainly to put at serious risk both Allied cohesion and, at the same time, the very credibility of our power to deter. All these consider-ations are at the heart of NATO's day-to-day business both at Evere and in capitals, and it may truly be said that strategy is under continuous review. Nothing has so far emerged which makes it seem in the least likely that there is a better one that none of us has so far thought of. Our minds, and happily there are many very good minds about in NATO, would be more usefully occupied in seeking ways to improve the manner in which our strategy is implemented. It should surprise no one to learn that this too goes on all the time.

CHAPTER XI

CRISIS MANAGEMENT

Crisis Management has, for no very good reason, been shrouded in some secrecy and not much discussed, with the result that some strange ideas have got about and the subject as a whole is regarded as too esoteric for public debate. This is not so, but if there is to be a sensible debate, with those concerned at least observing similar conventions, a certain amount of ground must first be cleared.

It is probably true that crisis management is, at one and the same time, a sort of science and a sort of art form. It is a sort of science because the tools of the trade and the methodology and technique of using them can be listed and described and a tolerable staff manual could be written on the subject. In short the mechanics can be taught and their use practised. But it contains, and by its very nature always will contain, elements of an art form, because it is in the end a matter of exercising judgement not only about facts but about things which are likely (or not) to happen because of those facts. This cannot be taught, and a tolerable staff manual could not be written about it. However even the art form can be practised, to the extent that the players can be exercised in weighing facts and potential developments which lead to the need to make decisions, and to foresee and elaborate the consequences which would or could flow from them, by devising plausible scenarios. In this way Ministers (nearly all branches of Government are or certainly should be involved), Commanders down to at least formation level and perhaps even to units, and officials from Ambassadors down to messengers, can be regularly confronted with simulated crisis conditions. During this process the tools of the trade can be tried for size and shape, and all elements of this particularly crucial form of management can be required to function in their actual role in a near approach to real-life and real-time conditions. This is a primary purpose of the major event held by NATO every year in the series of command post exercises which involves all levels of political and military control in the Alliance. They are sponsored in alternate years by the Secretary General and by SACEUR.

Ten years ago various experts protested against the theory of crisis management then put forward by Herman Kahn. According to him, all military conflicts below the threshold of total nuclear war should be regarded as crises and be dealt with as such, and the theory was expressed in his famous 'Escalation Ladder'. This, however, is unlikely to be acceptable for members of an alliance, because a nation hit by conventional attacks or even by small-scale selective nuclear strikes would always take this to mean war, and not just a crisis. This seems reasonable enough and to be demonstrated by the fact that it is quite normal for the public to speak of the Berlin crisis, the Suez crisis and the Cuba crisis, but of the Korean war, the Vietnam war and the Yom Kippur war. It may well be wise to assert at the outset that crisis prevention is not the same thing at all, important though it certainly is, being concerned much more realistically with the search for détente.

Having asserted what form of sport this is and some contrary thesis, it becomes at once necessary to define it, and this is easier said than done. A large number of definitions have been tried and each has some merit. For the purpose of examining crisis management here the definition of an American expert, Professor Lipson, seems handy, and in a different sense manageable: 'A crisis is a controversy between single governments, or groups of governments, over an issue which is deemed fundamental to the basic interests of one side or both. An unusual intensity of feeling is generated and there is a possibility that force may erupt. A crisis is managed if a solution acceptable to both sides is reached without resort to force. It is successfully managed if the underlying sources of conflict are removed for the future. Amending Clausewitz one can suggest that international politics consists of the prevention of war by other means.' It might even be helpful to turn the term 'crisis' back into its original medical meaning—namely 'a very serious illness rapidly cured'—by way of amending Lipson. Three things must remain excluded from such a definition of 'crisis' and 'crisis management': first, the solution of long-term political differences between states, because they form part of normal diplomatic relations; secondly, the elimination of tensions by the capitulation of one side, as of the Western powers *vis-à-vis* Hitler in the case of Czechoslovakia, because if one side simply gives up its vital political interests, this is not crisis management but defeat; and thirdly, the situation where a crisis ends in war and this is not a case for crisis management but for war management. Having established these elementary ground rules, it is now possible to treat the subject, bearing always in mind that even if it seems too simple a beginning, history has shown that the point of departure for crisis management is the perception that a crisis impends.

Before studying the NATO system, it seems necessary and appropriate to discuss briefly some philosophical differences in the approach to this problem by East and West. NATO has always believed that it is possible to find a policy for preventing war between the two alliances, and precisely this has been put into practice for the past thirty years. During this time there have been many crises. In some the two great Alliances were opposed, as over Berlin and in the Cuba affair, but others were of a purely internal character within one or other of them: in the East the various upheavals in Hungary, Poland, East Germany and Czechoslovakia, and in NATO the recurrent difficulties, even if of a different nature, on its southern flank, in the 'cod wars', and over France's decision to leave the integrated NATO military organisation.

In both alliances, external crisis management mechanisms began some years ago to function in a fairly reliable manner, even if using different techniques, but as for managing crises internal to themselves, decisive policy differences emerged between the two systems, based on their fundamentally different philosophies. For example, it was not Czechoslovakia's intention to leave the political and military system of the Warsaw Pact in 1968; the intention was much less dramatic and amounted to an attempt at only modest liberalisation, within the Warsaw Pact organisational framework. Nevertheless, Moscow regarded this as a definite crisis which had to be met with tanks, guns and aircraft. The crisis management instrument in this case was military force, and the Brezhnev Doctrine was born.

NATO reacted quite differently when France left the military organisation of NATO—although it was a serious blow to the military side of the Alliance and a damaging diminution of its political cohesion. This crisis was very skilfully managed by NATO and France through negotiations conducted with honesty and fairness on both sides. It resulted, as is well known, in the West using its management ability, in the move of Headquarters, the build-up of a new, functional military organisation, the introduction of a new strategy, the drafting of newly appropriate defence plans, and a changed political framework to exercise control of it all.

No doubt, the crisis management system in the Warsaw Pact serves to enforce Moscow's political will. It can, and has been, used internally as a means of suppressing the national interests of the non-Soviet members, and to this extent it corresponds to the classical concept of imperialist policy; there is hardly any obvious difference between the technique used by the Romans to keep their empire together and that enforced by the Soviet Union. In all cases where power is not voluntarily accepted but is grudgingly tolerated, in former times Legions— today Divisions—march out to ensure obedience and the maintenance of the system. This is a form of crisis management, if not a very elegant one.

It must be admitted that our Western system is sophisticated and difficult for a Soviet planner to understand. To deal openly with conflicts between different national interests in the public arena appears illogical to the Soviets, nor can they even feel sure whether a crisis will be met by individual national reaction or by a joint NATO response, because their own methods make it impossible for them to judge in advance whether the hawks or the doves will prevail. It is incomprehensible to the Communist way of thinking that the United States encourages NATO members actively to prosecute many of their individual interests, while at the same time sparing no effort to bring them together to play their collective part in NATO.

The Soviet crisis manager is only aware of the apparent

inherent contradiction in the NATO system, and—being a prisoner of his own system—he fails to realise that in a real crisis this contradiction disappears and gives way to solidarity. He also cannot understand the relationship between Western governments and public opinion. The Soviet planner is used to a system in which press opinion is identical with the views of his government, to such an extent that the inter-relationship between Western government activities and the press criticism which they provoke remains a closed book to him. For all these reasons, therefore, he can only react to this confusing picture by keeping himself in readiness for every and any possibility.

It may seem paradoxical that the closed system of the Warsaw Pact, at least in theory, is more easily calculable for a Western crisis manager, because actions are normally based on well-known tactics and obvious political aims. It is also, regrettably, possible to miscalculate this system. Certainly the construction of the Berlin wall as a Communist instrument of crisis management had not been foreseen by any Western governments, nor did many Western observers consider it possible that Communist governments would brutally suppress riots of their own working classes. And the soothing assumption that Soviet policy would always be guided by caution was starkly contradicted by Khrushchev's adventure in Cuba, and fifteen years later by his successors' in Angola. Perhaps the experience gained by both Alliances so far in the handling of crises leads to the conclusion that successful management of those crises in an East–West confrontation will be more likely to occur if first-class experts of the Western system are available in the East, and if the West can rely on experienced specialists of the Eastern system.

There are some other important influences to be considered surrounding the problem itself rather than its solution. NATO is confronted by a monolithic structure where decision-taking is both rapid and easy. We in the Alliance are dealing by contrast with fifteen sovereign states, of which twelve are in the integrated military structure, of varying political persuasions, with different ways of doing business, and in many cases geographically isolated one from the other. So even if we start off with the premise of a common approach and aim, it must be clear that unless each Government is fully and equally acquainted with the facts of a developing crisis situation, we are not going to get corporate agreement, let alone the complete unanimity that leads to rapid and positive political decisions. The matter of political determination will be treated in more detail later because it is first necessary to outline what has been done so far, and how the existing machinery has evolved.

It is a fact that so far in its history NATO has not had to grapple with a crisis in the terms of Lipson's definition. There have been isolated causes for alarm, but none of these, for reasons which may be a matter of opinion, involved the Alliance as a collective entity, even to the extent of ordering a Simple Alert. The fact that crises involving alert measures have not happened, or have been avoided, could be taken as a tribute to the success of the Alliance, but it could also, and less attractively, be attributed to a collective reluctance to take unpalatable decisions or to the absence of the machinery so necessary for rapid political consultation in fast-moving situations such as the Hungarian rising of 1956 and the invasion of Czechoslovakia in 1968.

If one considers the Soviets' aims and their growing capabilities, it is entirely possible that we could come to some sort of crisis situation again, and then NATO's aim must be to control it before it reaches proportions detrimental to Alliance interests. What means, then, are there to deal with such an eventuality? To see this matter in its proper perspective, it is necessary to look back a few years to the not too distant past. Until quite recently, the Alliance had no collective crisis management machinery at all. But the concept of flexibility in response changed the emphasis from a philosophy of all-out war with little or no warning (and hence little time or even need for collective consultation) to a strategy which envisaged that there would probably be a progressive deterioration in the politico-military situation before any attack were launched. During this period NATO's aim would be to take all possible steps to prevent hostilities actually breaking out and, if they did so, to control the response. Thus the introduction of this strategy brought with it the requirement for effective arrangements within the Alliance for crisis management, and anyone acquainted with national organisations in this field will recognise the scope and complexity of the problem thereby posed to fifteen sovereign and democratic Governments.

The arrangements we now have stem from the recommendations of the Special Committee of Defence Ministers which was established in 1966 under Mr. McNamara, then Secretary for Defense in the United States. The prime object of this Special Committee was to consider problems related to nuclear warfare, but on investigation it was found that many of the procedures and much of the machinery needed for consultation on the use of nuclear weapons were equally applicable over the whole range of political consultation and decision-making in a period of rising tension, and the outbreak of hostilities in conventional war.

Against this background we can now look at the essential machinery which has evolved so far, and which can be conveniently divided into the actual hardware and the arrangements and procedures for using it. Where physical facilities are concerned, the first requirement was for rapid, secure and reliable communications for the exchange of information and to further the process of political consultation and decision-taking. The NATO-wide communications system now links capitals with the Headquarters in Brussels and the three Major NATO Commanders in a system which is fully automated and computerised, and has a satellite capability. Allied to this communications system, which will eventually be merged into the NATO Integrated Communications System, is the secure telephone system—a highly sophisticated development, which really works, of the war-time 'scrambler'—which from modest beginnings five years ago is now planned to extend throughout the Alliance.

The next of the physical requirements was for a Situation Centre at the Headquarters in Brussels into which information from nations and the Major NATO Commanders could be fed, and there be collated, assessed and disseminated to similar coordinating elements in national capitals and NATO Commands. The Situation Centre, which has now been established, is equally responsible for the presentation of information at the NATO Headquarters to Ambassadors in the

Council/DPC and Military Representatives on the Military Committee.

In the last five or six years, a compendium of agreed procedures has been developed. The first concerns the exchange of information and intelligence, based on the premise that if fourteen or fifteen governments are to reach agreement on a common course of action, they must start from a common data base. The arrangements, which started in 1969, can be summarised as providing for intelligence coming from a capital to be transmitted to the NATO Headquarters in Brussels and the headquarters of the three Major NATO Commanders. Items of a particularly significant nature are disseminated immediately by capitals to all terminals on the NATO communications system.

The evaluation of military intelligence on an international basis, and the preparation of intelligence assessments by the Major NATO Commanders are particularly valuable, as there is a wide spectrum of talent and knowledge at our disposal. On more general politico-military developments, nations transmit to their partners in the Alliance, as well as to the Headquarters in Brussels and those of the Major NATO Commanders, their own continuing assessments of the situation. This procedure is founded on the principle adopted by Defence Ministers that to enhance timely and well-informed consultation in developing situations, member-governments should be prepared to exchange their own views with all other member-governments. It would, of course, be both illogical and positively dangerous if some nations were left in partial ignorance of, or out of touch with, all the relevant factors in a situation when corporate decisions had to be taken about it.

This exchange process provides a very necessary insight into the minds and attitudes of all member-governments and is now being complemented by machinery at the Headquarters in Brussels aimed at producing an agreed and continuously up-dated Alliance politico-military assessment of all aspects of a developing situation. Such an overall assessment would obviously be invaluable in time of tension since once a common interpretation has been achieved, it is much easier to agree about what should be done.

This leads to a consideration of how an agreed Alliance reaction is achieved in a real crisis, which must obviously be decided on an *ad hoc* basis depending on the circumstances. In deciding what to do, the Council or DPC has a fairly wide range of options. These vary from diplomatic and economic measures, through the spectrum of preparatory measures in the NATO Alert System, to agreed military contingency plans. Most diplomatic and economic measures would only be applicable at the lower end of the crisis spectrum, but this is not to underestimate their importance. If the situation escalates, however, the military options, such as the deployment of Immediate Reaction forces, the reinforcement of the flanks, the implementation of contingency plans or the implementation of force expansion plans, will of course loom ever larger in the minds of governments, and would be expected to find expression in the DPC.

In all this, one critical factor which must not be overlooked is the burden on the Council and DPC, which has become increasingly apparent during exercises. In a real crisis, the pressure on the Council and DPC would be very much greater, and Ambassadors or their deputies and the Military Committee would undoubtedly have to be in continuous session round the clock. Means must therefore be devised whereby certain decisions, especially those concerning the NATO Alert System, can be delegated to a multinational body below Council or DPC level. Some moves have already been made in this direction, but more remains to be done.

The consultations and the decision-taking processes so far described must constitute a very fine balancing act to prevent escalation on the one hand and provocation on the other. But the essential aim must be to ensure that adequate military measures to meet an attack are authorised in time to be effective if crisis management fails.

This leads naturally to the complex problem of warning time, and its relationship to the whole spectrum of crisis management as well as, rather more technically, to the NATO Alert System. Before we turn over some of these stones, it must at the outset be made clear that warning time must never be confused with the possible duration of conventional war-fighting, and the fact that it frequently is so confused is a fertile source of much ill-informed debate. Warning time has become, rather like nuclear weapons, what might be described as a sexy subject. It has attracted endless discussion which the participants thoroughly enjoy in the conviction that they, and only they, must be right despite the observed fact that, as in most other fields of human endeavour, this cannot be so. However, plainly some are more right than others and it is at least possible to articulate respectable projections of the likely course of events at various lengths of warning time, although it is not possible to be precise about the actual length of time which will be available. Thus estimates of the actual length of warning time, rather than of the circumstances to which this will give rise, will no doubt continue to be debated until it no longer matters. It will be noted that official estimates have been made both in capitals and at NATO Headquarters from time to time, but these have always been based upon certain reasonable but still hypothetical assumptions. At the time of writing (and, it could be held, for the foreseeable future) what is certain is that there will be some warning time and that it is likely to be measured in days rather than in either weeks on the one hand or hours on the other. The legion of unofficial estimates has ranged virtually from zero to infinity, usually to suit the axe which is being ground by the estimator whose main aim is to dignify his activity.

Early in 1977 NATO, and probably many others outside NATO, were suprised when a Belgian Major General published a book which contained, although he did not say so, a worst-case scenario in which what came to be called the 'standing-start blitz' took place with no warning at all, and resulted in the arrival of Russian armour at the Channel ports forty-eight hours later. His bizarre thesis received some apparent sprinkling of holy water from the almost simultaneous publication by a retired American Army Lieutenant General of a report indicating that NATO's forces in the Central Region were ill-equipped, undermanned and badly organised, and that a lightning thrust of this nature was entirely possible unless remedial action were taken. This wildly exaggerated assess-ment achieved some rather unjustified respectability by being accepted in large part by a prominent member of the United States Senate.

It is only worth mentioning these manifestations of axe-grinding (no doubt with the best possible motives) because the basic assumptions on which their hypotheses were erected are simply not true—which demonstrates the danger of amateur judgements on this highly critical element of crisis management. This 'standing-start blitz' notion, often referred to as 'surprise attack', is nevertheless worthy of serious but not hysterical attention. It is highly unlikely, but certainly not impossible, that NATO would be surprised, but there can be no doubt that the very considerable increase in all elements of the Warsaw Pact land and air forces deployed forward, coupled with the mal-deployment of our similar defences, makes an attack by their in-place forces a military possibility. This puts a further and still higher premium on the use of warning time, and gives considerable strength to the arguments for greatly improving all the means available to us which can speed up every stage of the readiness process.

Warning time is important not nearly so much to discover ('guess' would be a more accurate word) how many hours or days may be available, as to put in perspective what actually has to be done with such warning time as reasonable persons may count upon. First, warning time is essential for the military since, composed as the Alliance is of democratic sovereign societies, it will, for fairly evident political and social reasons, be slow to make up its corporate mind. And by the same token, for a defensive and (at least in peacetime) less powerful Alliance, warning time must be more important than it is for a superior power with the initiative in time and place and numbers. NATO depends, and always will depend, on the reinforcement of in-place forces not only on the flanks but also in the Central Region. This reinforcement must take the form of filling up gaps in the order of battle with reserves as well as by introducing extra-theatre elements especially for land and air forces; above all it must fill the logistic pipelines and all other forms of support. Thus for our military, warning time, if it is to be useful, must be turned into preparation time in order to make a smooth, quick and orderly transition, through the NATO Alert System mentioned earlier, from their peace-time posture to readiness.

It is of the utmost importance to appreciate that none of this can happen until the crisis is actually perceived on the political side and until the action which must be taken has, very quickly, been initiated. The importance of perceiving that a crisis impends has already been mentioned, but in the particular context of warning time, if this perception mechanism is not kept very sharp by education, training and practice, or if warning time turns out to be very short, a crisis may have been managed or muddled or missed before it is actually perceived.

It is, in practice, unlikely that the hope of the eternal procrastinators—that 'if you do not look at it too closely it will go away'—will be realised in these dire circumstances. It is therefore in this political arena that the real gut difficulty arises, and there can be no possible doubt that, operating as they do within the Allied democratic systems, Ministers will have to be extremely resolute and extremely courageous quickly to authorise those preparatory measures vital to the military, if public opinion is not solidly behind them. Thus greatly increased public understanding also involves an educative process which demands a continuing understanding of the issues which could be at stake in a crisis. The first political difficulty to arise is that of deciding whether the essential precautionary or preparatory measures are in fact provocative and thus likely, if taken, to heat up the crisis. Fortunately for all of us, history shows that this is unlikely, and during the lifetime of the Alliance there have been two classic examples where it was shown to be not provocative but vastly in the interests of deterrence: namely, the crises over Berlin and Cuba. If any doubt about this should linger in irresolute minds it may be observed that it is logically impossible for the same action to be both deterrent and provocative. And so we are back to the name of the NATO game, deterrence. An appreciation of this and of the crucial linkage, from the point of view of the Commanders, between warning time and its translation into preparation time are at the heart of the crisis management business.

It must emerge that NATO's machinery for managing crises involving the Alliance but not within it is now quite sophisticated and is being improved all the time. It is designed, above all, to arrive quickly at collective decisions with the spur of NATO's need to maximise preparation time through the vital ingredient of political will. And as well as the machinery, the professionals, in and out of uniform, whose business it is to oil it and drive it are by now also quite sophisticated and over the years have become quite numerous. If full use is to be made of these important advantages, it is important that all the players should be coached and given a great deal of practice at the game in the most realistic conditions that it is possible to simulate. Although monarchies have been accused of educating their princes too exclusively in the arts of warfare, it is suggested here that those who today exercise the awesome power of the monarchs of old are not always as well educated in crisis management as they should be.

CHAPTER XII

SOME PARTICULAR PROBLEMS

The book so far has been designed to set out the main boundaries
of the whole NATO problem and, in the sense of the basic-
English description of strategy, 'to define what the Alliance is
setting out to do and how it proposes to do it, in the light of
what it is given to do it with and what it is up against'. It has
been necessary for this purpose to linger over some notions
which are abstract like deterrence, some which combine
physical facts with abstractions like the threat and the nuclear
dilemma, and others which are purely factual like the machinery
of NATO government or the balance of conventional forces.
Running through each of these elements of NATO business
has been the dominant thread of political will and some of the
constraints which the internal problems of economics, politics,
technology and geography of the fifteen members impose,
because they are democracies, on the collective effort. It is, in
general, fair comment that each of these constraints (and there
are others) dilutes or diminishes the optimum approach to the
solution of truly Allied problems. By contrast none of them, so
far at least, has influenced in the smallest degree what the
Soviet authorities regard as the optimum solution to similar
Warsaw Pact problems.

It is now time to look more closely against this backcloth at a
selected few of the important problems with which the Council
and the Military Committee must grapple. No attempt is made
here to suggest any order of priority, because this is very
difficult and nearly always gives rise to argument which, while
interesting, frequently blurs what should be the hard outline
of the problems themselves. Moreover those which have been
chosen must all be solved, and solved simultaneously rather
than sequentially, if NATO is to stay successfully in business.
What can be said at once is that each of those discussed is

intimately connected with what are often referred to in the trade as 'the three Ds': deterrence, defence (forward and flexible) and détente. That many pressing problems have been left out will quickly become plain, nor is it here claimed that those included are the most important. Rather they have been selected as a representative cross-section of those which have real politico-military natures, and which have also attracted rather less public attention than they deserve.

As good a point of departure as any is the 'image' of NATO. This is the conventional shorthand for a very wide range of interlocking qualities and factors which make up the perception of the Alliance in our own hearts and minds—and eyes too— and in the hearts, minds and eyes of any likely opposition and of those aligned with neither East nor West who span the spectrum from benevolence to malevolence. To deal first with the family, it must be said that there is an extremely widespread ignorance of NATO affairs among the general public in every one of the fifteen member-countries. It is especially regrettable that this ignorance is to be found among many of those persons and groups of persons who should know better, including for example officers in the armed services, officials in central and local government, leaders in industry, commerce and the learned professions, important figures in the trade unions, and, most depressing of all, the media. This is bad news for us all, and arises from a failure to do enough to project this image nationally, which is where the responsibility has been laid by Governments. Certainly NATO Headquarters could do better, but within the club rules made by the 'Committee', the NATO Information Service does a respectable job. It is the more exasperating to those many servants of the Alliance at all levels, who serve in national and international positions, that a warm and benevolent attitude towards Defence in general and NATO in particular is invariably revealed by frequent and authoritative opinion polls in all member-countries. Plainly we must try harder, and it would neither cost much nor be difficult, but although several promising initiatives have been taken in the last ten years, all have quickly run out of steam. As in so many other aspects of our business, and indeed almost any other business, the lead must come from the top as a conscious act of policy with a committed determination to succeed. This has been, and still is, conspicuously lacking, though Ministers predictably say, and could just possibly think, otherwise.

Outside the family the image varies rather naturally according to the eye of the beholder. The important point for the Allies is that the facts of NATO life should be made available, in unambiguous terms, to all those (and there are more about than many people suppose) whose minds are not closed and who genuinely wish to know them. If this were done—and it is on the whole not done well and sometimes not done at all— their judgements might not be wiser but, *pace* Lord Birkenhead, they would be better informed and, because we have a good story to tell, that would certainly be beneficial. Facts, in short, are the key to this puzzle, both inside and outside the family. They need no embellishment and it is usually a blunder to try it. They would, to take one of the most obvious examples, make it luminously clear to even the dullest Russian (in the highly unlikely event of his being allowed to know them) that there was no chance whatever that the 'Revanchist German Army' with a strength of 400,000 and 3,000 tanks was about to attack the Soviet homeland defended by at least 1,000,000 men and 20,000 tanks. It would, in passing, do no harm to rub the noses of some of our own lunatic fringe in similar facts by stating them more loudly and more often in the West than we do.

In an earlier chapter it was remarked that money is not the root of much NATO evil, and it is not. But it is money, or what money can provide, which is at the root of many of our most difficult problems, and some discussion of the available resources will expose in a natural way the linkage between them. In very simple terms it cannot be denied that the Alliance is short of resources for the proper discharge of the Three Ds. Ministers have, in the last five years, repeatedly pledged themselves (and one must suppose this means their Governments), in the communiqués issued twice a year after their meetings in the Defence Planning Committee, 'to devote in real terms a steady amount, desirably increasing by up to 5 per cent a year, to Allied defence', but it must be stated flatly that this has not happened. One must also suppose that this pledge was not given 'wantonly, lightly or ill-advisedly', any more than it is in the Anglican marriage service, but it still has not been honoured. Some members have kept their pledge, though they are very few, and others have more nearly kept it than the remainder, but the nett result is that there are today fewer men, less money and less equipment than there were five years ago and could and should be now. This is bad news too. For the moment it must be realistic to suppose that, short of receiving some nasty fright, or a dramatic change in policy occurring for some nobler reason, NATO's resources year by year are unlikely to increase. This leads without undue mental strain to the conclusion that until wiser counsels prevail we must obtain better value, in terms of our objectives, for the money we have. There are many ways of doing this, which, taken together, are at the same time among the more important problems—and the bread-and-butter business—of the higher direction of NATO.

Infrastructure has the special connotation in NATO of those projects—sometimes activities—which are commonly funded for the general benefit of the Alliance. It includes fixed construction works of all sorts from aircraft shelters to underground headquarters, communication facilities in the widest sense, and improvements to airfields and ports and even to barracks, workshops and so on. Such projects are, of course, undertaken in all the member-countries. Infrastructure thus provides a special instance of the need for resources, of the effects of not having enough of them, and of some of the pressures which lead to this. It also illustrates what is, in a sense, a double problem in that the task of deciding what infrastructure is needed is by no means simple *per se*, but is immensely complicated once that need has been met by finding a year or two later that the expected resources are no longer available. It is a special instance in another respect in that it is a visible and tangible outward sign, and in a certain sense the only such sign, of the collective NATO effort and could, not too fancifully, also be regarded as a very important signal (as well as a sign) of Allied cohesion and solidarity. It is, regrettably, a highly contentious and time-consuming process to bring to a conclusion. Although the money at stake is very little in relation to the total Allied expenditure on defence (for example, the figure for 1978–9 is less than one-tenth of one per cent or one-thousandth of the sum of national defence budgets), it has proved impossible in the last five years to obtain more than about half of what the Military Committee has recommended after the most intense scrutiny of what the Major NATO Commanders have deemed essential. Finance Ministers appear quite unable (or, more likely, unwilling) to comprehend the consequent diminution of military effectiveness that this self-evidently causes, and much less to care about the damage it causes to the very spirit of cohesion on which the Alliance, in the end, depends. Regrettably this special problem, unlike most of the others which follow, is not amenable to more than cosmetic treatment by seeking better value for money because one must presume that even (or perhaps especially) a Finance Ministry official must know that to use cheaper or thinner concrete, or less concrete, on an aircraft shelter is a false economy.

Happily, the next clutch of problems presents clear opportunities for getting better value for money. Although many of the nationally generated constraints—especially in the economic, industrial, technical and occasionally secrecy (as opposed to security) fields—have to be overcome, they certainly can be overcome with determination at the top and a better understanding all the way down. Standardisation is the name of this part of the game, and although many enthusiastic hearts have become withered and cynical in its pursuit, that is absolutely no reason for giving up now. It must be said at once, though it is often overlooked, that the search is for standardisation in doctrine as well as in equipment. It is also important to deal, as briefly as possible, with some nomenclature because therein lies ample room for cross-purposes and misunderstanding. For this purpose, standardisation will be held here to refer to equipment, or doctrine, which is the same in whosever hands it may be or in whatever mind conceived it. It should be noted, in passing, that this is what obtains throughout the forces of the Warsaw Pact. Two steps along the road to standardisation are interoperability and compatibility, which are not only different from each other but both fall well short of standardisation itself, and the not uncommon failure to understand this (which sometimes appears deliberate) has made life even more difficult for those who have tried, and are trying, to bring it about.

Two other words creep frequently into standardisation talk, and have no business to be there: 'rationalisation' and 'specialisation'. Arbitrary definitions, again for the present purpose, will have to serve if for no other reason than the painfully observed fact that any agreed definition tends to attract as much discussion as the subject itself. These four terms apply almost entirely to equipment, although the first two have some relevance to doctrine. 'Interoperability' means very simply that one wireless set can talk to and be heard by another different one; that one air force's bombs can be hung on to and dropped by another's aircraft; that one ship may embark fuel from another even though their deck fittings are different, by the use of an adaptor; being able to use someone else's small arms ammunition from a different rifle; and that in the doctrinal sense a commander will get the same response from any national unit if he asks for fire support, air cover or ship bombardment. 'Compatibility' means that quite different equipment can work together by being capable of doing the same job, such as going at the same speed, firing ammunition which has the same effect, using fuel for vehicles which while not the same will still make them go, or offering equivalent protection. 'Specialisation' and 'rationalisation' refer essentially to tasks, and the former should be used in the sense that one country might specialise (but only for example) in making, or operating air defence equipment, or mine counter-measures vessels while deciding not to be in the business of anti-tank weapons or ship fire control. 'Rationalisation' tends to be used in the sense that common supply arrangements are made by one party on an agency basis for several others, operating transport or recovery vehicles on a pool basis, using the same accounting procedures, medical terms and treatment, and so on.

All these sub-cultures of standardisation have merit, though they have some disadvantages too. One serious disadvantage is that they take the practitioner's eye off the true objective and, because it is an easy way of avoiding some of the crunches on the way to real standardisation, is a rather attractive soft option and thus as dangerous as these always are. There is another disadvantage which could also be serious although so far it is more a lurking possibility than a reality. Some ardent proponents of specialisation have put about the notion that they might give up some field of military activity such as surface-to-air missiles or long-range maritime patrol aircraft in order to concentrate better on some other such as air superiority fighters or anti-submarine helicopters. This is a respectable proposition if, and only if, some other ally is prepared, so to speak, to undertake the reverse specialisation in the same time-scale. This is a very big issue, involving realistically an acceptance by both parties of a diminution in their national capability. The Alliance as a whole ought perhaps to undertake this but, certainly at present, it is far from ready for such a dramatic political change of course amounting, as it must, to acceptance of an actual diminution of sovereignty. In the absence of such agreement, if one member decides unilaterally to specialise in this manner, then either some other must 'pick up the tab' or a gaping hole will appear in the Allied order of battle. Although a good deal of preliminary skirmishing around this issue has taken place, NATO has not yet seriously addressed itself to what is an extremely awkward and difficult problem, but we will have to do so and better soon than too late. It is probable that this concept is not negotiable, and if careful examination shows this to be true then much time and rhetoric will be saved by saying so early rather than late.

The military advantages of standardisation hardly need explanation, since they cannot fail to simplify immensely the task of the Commander at any level, and of course that of his logistician. With true and effective equipment standardisation any field workshop would be able to repair any Allied vehicle or gun or anything else that battlefield maintenance may be organised to do. Any unit could obtain spare parts, more ammunition and more equipment from any national ordnance field park; all aircraft would burn the same fuel, have the same weapons and the same attachments for them, and could thus be re-armed and turned round at any airfield; and so through the maritime environment in the whole gigantic inventory of war material today. Nor does it begin to end there. Without attempting to complete the enormous catalogue, every soldier, sailor and airman would be operating the same kit and could, in principle, be trained or re-trained on it by any of his Allies in any Allied country. And so on, through the whole field of support right up to the battle area. The economic advantages would seem equally plain, certainly in the long term, but these regrettably have been obscured for many years by the short-term disadvantages and the actual difficulty of bringing it about. Ministers and Chiefs of Defence have been publicly united for a long time in their warm agreement, in principle, that standardisation is not only 'a good thing' but one which in the end has got to happen.

A succession of valiant and determined efforts have been, and continue to be, made to get this show on the road but they have all so far failed to get over the hump thrown up by pressures or constraints in the very powerful national industrial Establishments. The standard objection which these raise is that if standardisation is to be imposed they will all lose the design, the development and the production of their home-grown article and this, they persist, will lead to loss of technological expertise, to the emasculation of their defence-based industries, to significant unemployment and (very telling) to a dramatic loss of arms exports and thus of much-needed money across the exchanges. This tear-jerking scenario, it is clear, touches politicians on a number of deeply sensitive spots, and thus the 'hump' of what is, in plain terms, selfishness is made higher and wider and longer and then underpinned by political considerations. However, this fairy story, or perhaps horror story, is simply not true and a very large number of competent economists and industrialists are ready to prove it (this is not the place to do so).

There are some general observations to be made at this point. About half the Allies have no significant defence-based industry, and are in consequence what might be described as customers, and of the remainder two or three have a rather narrowly based defence industry able to design or manufacture (or both) a limited range of weapons systems or components.

These might be described as customers and specialist producers. Perhaps only the United States is a producer of the whole spectrum of war stores on the grand scale with a technological and industrial base probably as big as that of the rest of the Allies put together, and the United Kingdom still retains a very widely based ability over nearly the whole of the research and design, development and engineering and production spectrum. It is, among more compelling pressures, this very diversity of capability which makes agreement on how to proceed to eventual standardisation so difficult to achieve. To give added point to this rather gloomy assessment it has been truly said that NATO's forces are less standardised today than they were in the 1950s when all were almost entirely equipped with American or British equipment, and it is an observed fact that in our inventory we now find about fifteen different anti-tank weapons when three would do, more than thirty combat aircraft types when perhaps six would do, four quite different tactical (battlefield) communication systems, at least four different new-generation tanks and hardly any inter-navy standardisation at all—to give half a dozen examples out of perhaps 500.

The news, despite all this, is now not wholly bad. It is a welcome sign of grace that hardly anyone in the business today disputes (it has been doggedly disputed for years) that this sort of thing simply will not do, and particularly—to go back to where this passage began—no doubts remain about the overriding importance of getting better value for the same or less money. Some specific and useful initiatives have broken surface in the last three years and may well be said to have taken root, although they are still tender plants which need constant care and attention and, almost certainly, cannot be forced. Not the first, in time, but potentially the first in importance is what has come to be known as the 'two-way street'. By this is meant a flow of equipment purchases in both directions across the Atlantic. The United States Administration has shown, in spite of the great power and influence of its industrial lobby, remarkable determination to get the traffic flowing, against the historical tide, from East to West. The 'Buy-American' Act has been amended (not without considerable difficulty) to enable their Secretary for Defense to procure European equipment, provided (and these are entirely reasonable pre-conditions) that it meets the operational requirement, that the price is competitive and that delivery can be guaranteed at the time when it is wanted. Shopping lists have been drawn up for the medium and long term of likely categories in which the Europeans can meet these requirements. Traffic has actually started to flow, quite recently, along this street by American purchases of a useful, though still fairly small, range of equipment. There have, of course, been setbacks which have not only been disappointing but have created, at the time, some very hard feelings; and it is only necessary to mention the failure of Anglo–US, Anglo–German and German–US discussions on the next main battle tank, and the collapse of the very imaginative (even if extremely expensive) attempt to create a NATO-owned Airborne Early Warning and Control System in this latter category, to show that we are still a long way from home.

An essential feature of this 'two-way street' must, almost by definition, be that at each end of it there is an industrial organisation capable in the widest sense of building the traffic which it is hoped will flow along it. This means, in practice, sharply improving the European end of it in quality and in production capacity—which in turn demands that the European producers must organise themselves collectively to deliver. This has not been easy for all the reasons already mentioned, and it still is not easy, but here too some important work has begun and is being pursued. The Eurogroup, which at first was mainly occupied with harmonising policies, has proved, after its small beginnings, to be an ideal clearing-house for this new task which it is tackling with energy and growing enthusiasm. It does not, for this or any other purpose, include the French, which—certainly in this field of endeavour (as indeed in all others)—is unfortunate. The French defence industry has a long and successful history, it is by European standards large and diverse and of high technological quality, and it should, for these and other different but equally important reasons, desirably form an important component of the European matrix. However, the industrial lobby reservations already enumerated are all present but even to an exaggerated degree in France (especially the arms export lobby), and they are further compounded by much deeper political reservations, which created and maintain the unique position which the French Allies have chosen to occupy in our military affairs. They have, for example, publicly stated that they are not interested in standardisation (and not because it is a 'franglais' word) and have sometimes even gone further in suggesting quite incorrectly that this represents a European 'sell-out' to American industry. One hopes that this attitude will change under the stark reality of the fact that they too are driven by the imperative of getting better value for money, and in the meantime no efforts have been spared by the North Americans and their European friends to bring them fully into the act. There are already some hopeful signs that this may come about, such as the formation of an *Ad Hoc* Group (the capitals are intended) at Evere reporting directly to the Council, of which the French are full participating members, but whose terms of reference are, at the request of the French, confined to inter-operability. It has already done some useful work in this narrower field, which is now being complemented by the Independent European Programme Group set up in 1976, which also includes the French and which is tackling what might be called the foundations of the European end of the 'two-way street'; and does deal with standardisation problems. This can only be regarded as encouraging, and even though both developments are in their early days they can justifiably be described as a breakthrough.

To round off this somewhat lengthy excursion into standardisation, we need to return briefly to its application to doctrine. Doctrine is in many respects less difficult to standardise than equipment, mainly (if rather cynically) because it does not cost much money, and the industrial and resulting political constraints hardly apply. It may not be too parochial to suggest that it is also made easier because it is on the whole a matter for professionals, and military ones at that. There are however some pressures of different kinds which have to be overcome, and it has proved a slow—although steady—business. There exist, in the armed forces of each Ally, strong folk-memories of wars in which they have been involved and national analyses of their successes and failures, together with lessons learned from other wars. By no means all of these have equal application (or sometimes any application) to the defence of the NATO area. It is worth observing that the security thinking upon which Soviet forces are based, their equipment and deployment and doctrine, derives directly from their historical experience that God (or His Soviet substitute) really is on the side of the big battalions, and they have believed this since the time of Catherine the Great. Their military strategists have always held that only a considerable superiority over their opponent could ensure their country's safety; even in defence against the advance of Napoleon, General Kutusov always evaded battle unless he outnumbered the French by at least two to one. The rightness of this belief was underlined for them in the Second World War, particularly when the Nazis reached Stalingrad and the outskirts of Moscow within weeks of the assault beginning.

To a fortunately lesser extent this folklore syndrome has applied to NATO. For example, it is still in evidence in the deeply-held belief of many of the Generals in the US Air Force that their years of bitter experience in Vietnam read across to the European theatre. Because almost every single aspect of that war was totally different from any possible future war in Europe, hardly any of their Allies share this view, and to a smaller extent this applies across the board on which the game of war will in future by played in earnest, should it come. Good progress has, beyond question, been made by the Allied navies, armies and air forces, and of this the outward and visible sign is always first to be sought (and is now found) in the harmonisation of communication methods, procedures and material. This has on its heels the widespread acceptance of standard units of command, of levels of command and even tactics down to unit level. Many of those in charge of these events, particularly when in command, would like to move faster, but it is likely that short of the spur of actual war (when it would probably be too late anway) it is best in this matter to make haste slowly. It has been agreeable to note that discussions on doctrine go on all the time, at all levels, in the field and at the higher seats of Defence learning. Of this possibly the most successful manifestations are the study periods at Command Headquarters where all concerned can get down to teasing out the strands of some particular scenario problem in the search for the best approach, as well as a common one. On a much larger canvas, very detailed analyses have been made nationally, and by the Military Committee, of the Yom Kippur war in 1973 which yielded a dozen lessons of direct importance to NATO, despite the great differences in terrain, the size of the forces and the political background. Particularly in the armour versus anti-armour field, in the issue of air superiority and its derivatives of surface-to-air missiles and air superiority fighters, in logistics, in the use of warning time (almost the only thing really badly handled by the Israelis), and in the attrition of every sort of war stock, NATO has had to re-think some of its doctrine and re-emphasise other aspects in the light of that short but intense conflict.

All this is good news, and the doctrines which have emerged are constantly under test, refinement or alteration by the very large programme of exercises which take place all the time and in all the elements, under NATO sponsorship or even in many instances under national arrangements and organisation. This exercise programme almost certainly attracts less attention from the Council than it should, if for no other reason than that it is a very visible sign (and one invariably and carefully observed and monitored by the Warsaw Pact) of our deterrence. It is also highly important, outside its evident military utility, as a reassurance—particularly to those on the Flanks who feel lonely—and as an equally visible demonstration of political cohesion. It can also, in a smaller way, sometimes demonstrate a lack of cohesion, usually for 'special-case' reasons when political approval for an Allied exercise is withheld because some countries do not like their ships to visit Gibraltar, or alternatively Spain, or others cannot accept live-firing areas which offend their farmers, or low-flying air missions which keep the children awake or frighten their grandparents. These may seem very trivial when set against the magnitude of NATO's endeavour but they are examples, which are not only real but frequent, of a political failure to understand that unless the armed forces are allowed to practice their profession, not only will they become less and less good at it but they will be aware of that fact, and the high morale which is an absolutely fundamental ingredient of deterrence will quickly be lowered.

In spite of these artificial difficulties, NATO exercises have greatly expanded in both scope and scale under the stimulus of successive Major NATO Commanders and their subordinates, and in their knowledge that they have been able to count upon the unswerving support of the Military Committee and a sympathetic, if sometimes nationally constrained Council, which is officially and expressly responsible for approving the programme as a whole. Maritime exercises have always gone well and are now more frequent and more imaginative, thanks in no small part to our careful observation of Soviet maritime exercises of which the largest in their history took place under the name of *Okean* '75 in that year. Exercises by the Air Forces have also been continuous in all the many facets of their exacting task, so as to keep closely in line with the new opportunities presented by their rapidly advancing technology and, what is perhaps of even greater relevance, with the advances in tactics and weapons systems employed by the land and sea forces over which they operate. For fairly obvious reasons it is less easy to stage large-scale land forces exercises, but today much can be very realistically simulated. Formations up to battle group or division level can be and are regularly deployed in the field, and while the tactics of corps and army groups are important, their command and control are paramount and this is not inhibited by space or time or safety constraints. It has also been easy and welcome for the political and military authorities at Evere and in capitals to 'plug in' to such parts of this combined enterprise as they can make time for and from which they derive much practice and benefit. The most significant advance in the whole history of NATO's exercise programme began in 1975 (and is quickly being further developed) when SACEUR took the initiative in putting together under one umbrella a large number of regular exercises, customarily held in the early autumn, by arranging that NATO exercises and national exercises should be complementary in general scenario and timing. Thus, without the training cycle of his own Commanders or of national Commanders being inhibited, one major Alliance-wide land–air event of great military and political importance is created instead of many small ones which would have passed unnoticed and failed to contribute to the sum of NATO preparedness, or its visibility.

Turning sideways, in the sense that it is neither up nor down the scale of importance either in itself as a NATO problem or as a fruitful source from which much better value for money can be obtained, we come now to the last subject to be tackled in this chapter, and that is the very complicated one of logistics. It is necessary once again to define what is meant here by the word, so as to limit the area of discussion to reasonably modest proportions. It will be held that 'logistics is the function of equipping armed forces with what they need, for all the stages from peace to war, for supplying them and re-supplying them with things and with people', but even that is too wide an area to cover towards the end of an already long chapter. It remains true, as has been remarked earlier, that if this function fails, the most brilliant Commander with the bravest troops will certainly not succeed.

Logistics got off to a bad start in NATO because the founding military fathers decided that 'logistics is a national responsibility', and nearly (but not quite) all the difficulties over them which have since arisen flow from that briefly stated mistake. What they should have said—and since they were experienced and sensible men, they may even have meant to say it—was that 'it is a national responsibility to discharge the logistic function for their forces under [or 'to be under'] NATO command to the satisfaction of their Allied Commander'. There is a great deal more than semantics here, and the abridged version, which remains graven on NATO tablets, has given every single Ally at one time or another license to fail to do what the longer version requires. In fact it has not only given them licence not to do it, but nearly all of them have used the licence nearly all the time. The mistake (it undeniably was a mistake) almost certainly arose from similar considerations to those which have already been outlined at some length under standardisation, and it must be remembered that when this *diktat* was formulated, the process of military integration, which had never before been attempted on the NATO scale, was in its infancy. The small national forces had been supplied with relatively large war stocks to eat down or wear out, only the American and British defence industries were functioning on a useful scale, and the last thing on which Governments wanted to spend desperately needed recovery money was logistics for their armed forces. These and other constraints continued to apply in the minds of those responsible for a long time after common prudence had demanded that the support pipeline should be re-started, re-furbished, reorganised and subjected to the same rigorous scrutiny as was being applied to those same aspects of the teeth arms.

One important influence on this state of mind and the state of affairs it produced, was the fact that in all the Services in all the NATO countries the logistic function was carried out, as in many cases it always had been, by a special branch of the Staff rather than by the operators. This is still true today. It is a normal failing of those Commanders and what in British terms are their 'G' staff (the operators) to allow the 'Q' staff (who are 'mere' suppliers) to get on with the rather dull and grubby details of boots and 'baccy and bullets until the awful realisation dawns that not only have the 'Q' staff not produced them but they have not actually been told what is required. Countless people will not agree with this dismal analysis, but even they can hardly disagree that if the same time and talent had been devoted to the tail in the last thirty years as has been devoted to the sharp end, there would be many happier men than can be found today among those with the ultimate responsibility for the whole deterrent. This is not a new phenomenon, for without the astounding energy and unusual brilliance of the Duke of Wellington's Quartermaster General, the young Canadian Sir William de Lancey, his army and its kit would never have got into the line to start the battle, and Waterloo would never have been won.

At all events NATO is now well aware that we must do much better and do so quickly. Three useful lines are being pursued separately, but simultaneously, within a general Allied—if not yet a nationally accepted—view of logistics: first, that it is very much behindhand and thus diminishes deterrence; secondly, that it is a command function to state the requirements; and thirdly that it is at the heart of Alliance business, and must not and cannot be left only to capitals. A promising start has been made at Evere on a fresh approach, which has taken the form of separating what have been called 'consumer' and 'producer' logistics and then having the quite different range of problems which each respectively throws up attacked by suitably qualified experts in each field. Such a separation is bound to be arbitrary but it need not be contentious, nor need it prevent a topic from being moved from one group to the other or, in strictly limited instances, from being shared. Consumer logistics embraces in principle the function of putting the troops (in the generic sense) into position and there marrying them to their equipment and then keeping both topped up to establishment. Producer logistics, which comes both before and after this, is the function of deciding what kit— not only weapons systems but petrol oil and lubricants, food, clothes and accommodation—the troops need, and then providing it to the logistician behind the consumer. This is a big function because it goes as far back in time as the staff requirement for an item of equipment needed ten years later. Treated in an Allied framework, as it should be, it will involve very difficult problems of harmonising the actual requirement and then harmonising the time-scale at or within which it is provided. Most of the difficulties encountered along the road to standardisation are also met along the logistic road. It is gratifying to record that in the space of the last three years steady progress has been made in developing the machinery for tackling these two aspects of the logistic problem, and as confidence in the concept grows, so is progress likely to accelerate. Although it would be misleading to imply that anything more than a good start has been made, or that there is less than a very great deal yet to be done, there are sober grounds for believing that this twenty-five-year-old logjam has started to break up.

The third line is in the very wide field of re-directing the present efforts devoted to Civil Emergency Planning. Until recently most of this was done nationally with some bilateral or multilateral consultation, and a little was done by an understaffed and almost powerless Committee at Evere. One stubborn obstacle to progress here has been the different conceptions of the role of these planners in our various countries, some focussing on passive defence, evacuation, refugees and the like, while others were primarily involved in the military use of civil resources. In the worst instances, a clearly defined sense of direction or purpose was completely lacking. It must be totally clear that our military machine could never be capable of the consumer logistic task unaided, and that while it is easy to integrate the civilian organisations with those of the military in Warsaw Pact countries, the very nature of our democratic systems makes it intensely difficult for NATO to do so.

This is, of all the many which are so described, perhaps the truest and most tangible politico-military interface in the business. In the West the military are compelled to use civil aircraft, merchant shipping, civil pipelines, civil railways and autoroutes and the rolling stock on them, civil post, telephone and telegraph organisations, and so on through the gamut down to the traffic policeman and the farmhand. There has been inadequate coordination of these widely varying activities and facilities, not least because they are under national control and that control is shared, typically, among several ministries though not among the same ones in each country. Consequently it has been very difficult for Evere to enter this complex system. But here too the last two or three years have seen some useful progress, starting—as it should have done years ago— with a systematic drive to identify the separate strands, to quantify what has to be moved along what routes, to pin responsibilities firmly where they belong and to generate a dialogue between the Commanders and those who control the means of giving them what they want. It is not too optimistic to assert that the Alliance has reached nearly the end of the beginning and that good ideas are now widely shared about how to go forward. For go forward we must if our war-fighting capability is to be enhanced and our total deterrent to be believed.

These, then, are the sort of current and future problems with which the Alliance must, and does, grapple daily. Certainly they will not go away, and even when (perhaps one should say 'if') they are solved, there will certainly be others no less testing to take their place. In the final chapter, 'The Way Ahead', some of these, together with others, will be discussed with a view to suggesting how they might be better attacked than they are today.

CHAPTER XIII

DÉTENTE

Détente is certainly a problem, and a very special and intractable one at that. Although it is not a truly NATO problem, being much more a matter for the individual members, it is—because of its nature and the important effects it has already had, and because of the even more important ones which it could have in the future—highly desirable that NATO should arrive at a collective view, or at least a joint view, on how to deal with it. For this reason, and also because it is different in kind rather than in degree from those examined in the chapters between which this one is sandwiched, it is expedient to treat it—in so far as this can be done at all—separately.

It has been necessary elsewhere in this book, for the purpose of limiting the argument to manageable proportions, to postulate some arbitrary definitions. This is more than usually necessary in any discussion of détente—which presents quite major difficulties because outside these covers the word has been so frequently and so widely used over several years by so many people that there is clearly no formula which would stand even a sporting chance of general acceptance. It must surely mean something like 'the process of reducing (international) tension', and that might serve here as a point of departure. Even this, to be useful, begs two other related and equally basic questions: 'What tension, and what causes it?' and 'What is meant by "process" in this context?' It is in the process, and the results which it is thereby hoped to achieve, that we find one perception in the East and another in the West which are different to the point of incompatibility. While the Eastern perception is common to all those using it (because it is received wisdom), there is an honest lack of agreement about it in the West.

Détente has been described* as 'a diplomatic term denoting the attempt at establishing a situation of peaceful co-existence, with a growing level of fostered interdependence and co-operation between sovereign states in their international relationships', and as 'the attempt to lessen tensions between powers'; while co-existence has been held to mean 'a gradually increasing identification of certain interests between two or more otherwise antagonistic concepts of the organisation of society'. These would seem tolerable formulations on which to base a serious business discussion of the subject were it not that nearly all the many words of which they are made up are differently interpreted almost wherever they are used, which is why the search for definitions of this abstract notion has been and will continue to be a sterile exercise. It is also the main reason why progress in reducing international tension has been so painfully and disappointingly slow.

Tension undeniably exists and, strangely, continues to exist—among other reasons, simply because these words and all the others so far used here and elsewhere really do mean something different in the East and in the West, especially to the super-powers. For example, peaceful co-existence as a concept is enshrined in the Soviet Union as 'struggle'—class struggle or national liberation struggle—but détente is not enshrined there at all. Indeed, when Brezhnev said in 1976: 'Détente does not and cannot in the least degree rescind or change the laws of the class struggle', he was only underlining what Khrushchev had said twenty years earlier: 'Peaceful co-existence means nothing less than the continuation of the international class struggle with the ultimate aim of Communist victory everywhere in the world by all means at the disposal of the Socialist camp.' It would perhaps not be a dangerous oversimplification to suggest that most of the West would accept, as a description of the notion of détente (and co-existence too although it is not much used by us), language such as 'a willingness on the part of basically incompatible political systems to develop a level of co-operation which will enhance international stability and security'. It is these fundamentally

* At an Anglo-German conference in Brussels in 1976.

different perceptions, which arise from ideologies which are more than fundamentally different but are actually opposed, which make any orderly discussion of détente so difficult and, more important, the process of actually achieving it very much more so.

It should not be thought that the achievements so far are insignificant, for despite these difficulties they are not unimpressive, and quite a long list of successful attempts to promote détente can be recorded, including Treaties—or less formal but none the less binding Agreements—on Austria, the Antarctic, Outer Space, Nuclear Testing, and Fishing *inter alia*. It has been said that the search for détente, of which these are some successful examples, flows from the fact that 'the girdle of the Cold War has become too uncomfortable over the years and people want not just to loosen it but to take it off entirely'. This is in very large measure true, at least in the West. What is certain is that these and other agreements are not about the meaning of détente, but are simply the outward and visible signs of the search for it, and any misconception on this point (whether real or contrived) could be highly dangerous, with a boomerang effect for NATO. They could, specifically, be held up to the public gaze as actual evidence that dangers were going away, and thus give licence to another soft option for spending less on our security. This has, to an extent, already occurred in some Allied countries where there has been an actual impact on their respective defence policies—certainly without justification on account of anything which has actually happened or which any informed observer thinks is likely to happen. Those who believe, or affect to believe, the contrary must be made to answer two questions. First, has détente or any aspect of it induced the Soviet Bloc to cut back on its military programme? And secondly, did détente have any restraining influence on the Soviet Bloc's brazen interference in the affairs of Angola (and the Horn of Africa)? If these people should say 'Yes' to either question, they must be given the lie before such a frivolous and irresponsible view gains any credence.

Yet NATO is deeply involved, and has been from its formation, in the search for détente—at least, in the sense in which it is understood in the West. The evidence is there, for all who

are ready to rely on fact rather than on fancy, in the Harmel
Report, in the Ottawa Declaration, in the Reykjavik Signal and
in the very Treaty itself, all of which were discussed in the
first chapter. What is of the highest importance, bearing in
mind what has been said on the different perceptions of it in
East and West, is to remember above all that détente can only
be approached, by NATO, from a position of strength. Mr.
Callaghan put it very neatly when he was the British Foreign
Secretary by saying: 'Her Majesty's Government attaches high
priority to the improvement of East–West relations and to
détente, but in doing so [it] acknowledges that it is the strength
and security of the NATO Alliance which has dispersed the
atmosphere of open confrontation, and it is from this basis that
the search for détente must proceed.' These wise words should
illuminate all NATO thinking on the subject.

It is in fact precisely in this spirit that the Allies have
approached and conducted their discussions with the East on
Mutual and Balanced Force Reductions (MBFR) in Vienna,
now over four years old, having made a pre-condition of their
strategy and tactics alike that 'there should [as a consequence]
be no diminution of Allied security'. The initial reaction of the
Soviets to the Reykjavik Signal was characterised by great
reluctance, and it took them nearly six years to come to the
table; and since they did so their contributions have on the
whole been declamatory or legalistic, whereas the West has
resolutely addressed the military power of the two sides as the
likely source of conflict, and because of this has tried hard to
reduce it. This difference of approach, also, is basic and is the
main reason why the negotiations have dragged on for so long
with so little to show for all the time and effort they have
consumed. These differences of approach might be conveniently summarised before we look at them rather more closely,
by suggesting that it is the Western view that the present
military disequilibrium can only be restored to a tolerable
balance by reducing the Soviet superiority in offensive capability, while the Eastern approach is to preserve the present
ratio of power but at a lower level of men and equipment. In
the world of semantics these two widely different notions could,
without grave violence being done to the language, both be

held to lead to 'Force Reductions' which are 'Mutual' and which are 'Balanced', but the Eastern reading of the rubric is not at all what the Allies had in mind when they coined the description ten years ago. Beside the underlying incompatibility of these two theologies, the very question of the basis of comparison has bedevilled discussion at Vienna to the point where it has now become a very esoteric discipline in its own right, and shows hardly any sign of ever reaching a solution or, put another way, of ever arriving at a point from which meaningful discussion of actual reductions could start. It is unnecessary here to go into the detail of the disagreements about how to exchange data—or even what the data mean—or to discuss the actual proposals and counter-proposals or the reasons for their invariable rejection, because these have been voluminously documented in the special literature devoted to them. It is nevertheless beyond question that the Allies have tried hard to budge this so far immovable object in the general interest of reducing tension, but unless there is some movement fairly soon it may be, in very fact, counter-productive for us to continue. One gratifying aspect of what would otherwise be a rather dismal picture is that the negotiations themselves have been well conducted by NATO, with strategy being determined by the Council and the tactics dealt with by our Delegations in Vienna in an exemplary manner at each end. This has greatly added to the cohesion of the Allies generally and to their mutual confidence, well beyond the limits of MBFR.

Any discussion of détente without reference to the Strategic Arms Limitation Talks (SALT) and the Conference on Security and Cooperation in Europe (CSCE) would be incomplete. SALT, as is widely known, are a bilateral negotiation between the super-powers in which NATO plays no corporate part, although the Council is regularly informed by the United States of its intentions before each round, and of the results afterwards. CSCE, first at Helsinki and since at Belgrade, has not been a NATO affair either, although the Council has kept a very close eye on all the detail, and the Fifteen have sought, nearly always successfully, to harmonise their national approaches. Both these enterprises are designed to contribute to détente, however one defines it, and in principle at least, each should do so in large measure. That neither has yet done so is due to all the same reasons as those which illustrate the dissimilar perception of what the word and process actually mean.

It remains to mention some perceived obstacles to détente, and at least one potential danger to the Alliance in its pursuit. It has already been remarked that nothing should be done in aid of détente which diminishes Allied security, but there is a real danger that its more ardent proponents may be too anxious for success to maintain the agreed Western precondition. In particular, force reductions made unilaterally outside the context of MBFR would gravely weaken the position of our negotiators and at the same time would encourage the East in its recalcitrance. The less obvious obstacles to achieving the détente which NATO seeks may for convenience (although they have no other similarity) be described as destabilising factors, of which a few examples will now be given. Very high on any list must come anything which lowers the nuclear threshold. Several such factors have already been so labelled here, of which a reduction of our conventional forces below a critical level is probably the most obvious. The introduction of new and not fully evaluated weapons systems, such as the mobile intermediate-range ballistic missile by the Soviets or the Cruise missile or enhanced radiation weapons (the so-called neutron bomb) by the Americans, are highly de-stabilising possibilities, as would be the deployment by either side of a really efficient anti-ballistic missile system or a technological breakthrough in submarine detection. The Soviet civil defence programme, if driven through to a conclusion, would gravely alter the balance of military power by non-military means, as would projection by them of political influence by military means elsewhere in Southern Africa, as was done in Angola. On the NATO side any loosening of our political cohesion, whether through quarrels between members, lack of a resolute collective attitude to Euro-Communism, unilateral reductions in contributions to our whole deterrence or any other cause, is another potentially de-stabilising element.

Given that NATO is pledged to the concept of détente, these are some of the difficulties that must be squarely faced if they are to be overcome without loss to our objectives. It may well be that more attention should be paid to making sure that de-stabilisation never starts before too much attention is paid to new horizons. Whether this is generally agreed or not, there can hardly be any reasonable doubt that the only soft options here are as dangerous—albeit superficially attractive—as they are everywhere else. There is certainly nothing in the Final Act done at Helsinki, in the negotiations which it concluded, or in its aftermath which should persuade the Alliance to lower or reduce its deterrent shield.

CHAPTER XIV

THE WAY AHEAD

Earlier chapters promised a return to some of the problems
which NATO faces today, and a look at some fresh ones, so that
indications might be given of different ways of tackling them or
a re-direction of our approach which could lead to earlier or
better deployment of effort. It has been asserted more than once
that hardly any of our problems can today be treated as
exclusively political or military or economic, though in each
problem one of these factors is usually dominant. It may be
remarked in passing that this now undisputed fact of NATO
life would make it inconceivable today for the Council and the
Military Committee and their respective staffs to be physically
separated as they were until just over ten years ago.

One element which can lend itself to some degree of separation is organisation, even though the interface between the
various family trees must be very solid if the total enterprise is
to succeed. Starting with the political side of the house, there
has undoubtedly been a perceptible diminution in the attention
paid by the Council to Defence subjects and a marked increase
in that paid to all the other matters with which the Permanent
Representatives are concerned—the reasons for this have already
been touched upon. This is not because of the existence of the
Defence Planning Committee, because it consists of the same
people (less two) as the Council, nor is it because the problems
of the Military are now any less difficult, but the relative
frequency of their meetings leaves no doubt that such a
diminution has occurred. To give substance to this, the records
show that in typical recent years the Council met four or five
times more often than it did as the DPC. The reasons for this
do not matter greatly, although it must be said that stark fear
has diminished and it may be suggested (perhaps harshly) that
Ambassadors prefer talking about ideas (which has been their

137

life-work) to talking about things. What does matter is that this makes life much more difficult than it need be for the Military Committee. This is particularly noticeable in Ministerial meetings; the level of debate is much higher—because it is better prepared—at the average meeting of Foreign Ministers than at the meeting of their colleagues for Defence.

It cannot be regarded as satisfactory for an Alliance pledged to Deterrence, Defence and Détente to focus too closely on one of these elements at the expense of either of the others. Nor can it be satisfactory for either of these highest-level bodies to meet in the physical absence of their colleagues for Finance since most of the end-products of their deliberations will depend for their implementation on money. There can be no reasonable doubt that our affairs would be better managed if Foreign and Defence Ministers met jointly for at least one day at their twice-yearly meetings and if they were joined at one of their meetings by the Finance Ministers. If this were done, not only would discussion be better informed and better balanced but commitments entered into would be harder—and harder to wriggle out of. Moreover, the spirit of such joint Ministerial meetings would inevitably (and greatly to our advantage) have to be reflected in the permanent Council and DPC discussions at Evere. There is a further possibility, which has been suggested more than once, namely the establishment at Headquarters of joint meetings of the Military Committee and the DPC. This undoubtedly has some superficial attractions. In practice, because much of the Military Committee's work is to prepare papers for political consideration or approval, the advantages are more apparent than real, but there does exist a range of topics which might well make this desirable, and no harm would be done by giving it a trial.

As for the military organisation there can also be no reasonable doubt that this could well be improved, in military terms, although there are important political constraints. The lines of responsibility between the Military Committee and the Major NATO Commanders are clearly established and have stood the test of ten difficult years. The role of the Military Committee has not been tested in tension or war, but it is regularly and frequently exercised and no obvious flaws have been revealed.

It is over the actual Command Structure, which for this purpose must include the Chairman of the Military Committee and also the Military Representatives, that there is room for reasonable doubt that we have the best answer. Indeed the Military Committee formally proposed in 1976 that the Command Structure should be thoroughly examined, but the Council held that it was not then politically expedient. At the top, there are several possibilities, all of which have been suggested at one time or another though none in formal proposals. These have ranged from abolishing the Military Committee altogether and giving each national delegation a 'military adviser', through combining the posts of SACEUR and of the Chairman of the Military Committee, to making the Chairman a Deputy Secretary General who might even take charge of the permanent DPC. And there have been various permutations of these widely differing notions. The Chairman is, by definition and recognition, the star at the top of the NATO military tree (though it is not usually expressed so poetically). However, contrary to the classic definition of a harlot, he has immense responsibility but very little power. Even though his hands may be on the levers of power, he can only move them by persuasion and by personal influence which flow in equal measure from his personality and his office. This is plainly not satisfactory in theory even though it has worked well enough in practice, and the military organigram would undoubtedly be improved if his special position were to be more formally delineated so as to reflect its realities. The Chairman would undoubtedly be of more use to the Secretary General and thus to the Council and DPC and through them the Alliance (even though he is now the only military person with a seat at their table) if he were formally charged with presenting the best International military advice, generated by what would have to become 'his' International Military Staff, with due account taken of national differences of opinion. Because, to a remarkable extent, there is seldom any important difference of military opinion, such national reservations are invariably due to political (including financial) reasons. Logically, they might be better expressed, argued and resolved at the political level than, as now, by diluting the military wisdom available collectively from the dozen

Allied Chiefs of Defence. This general line of thought is certainly shared by past Chairmen of the Military Committee, and has been expressed in formal reports to the United States Secretary for Defense, and through similar channels elsewhere. To make this change would, without doubt, involve a major upheaval with very strong political side-effects, and before putting it in hand it would certainly be prudent to seek a 'Command Structure' package of which this would be a major part. Big changes of this nature are seldom welcome, and can always be deemed to be untimely for one reason or another, but the arguments against at least examining the problem are on the whole pretty feeble.

At the next layer down come the Major NATO Commanders and there is neither much wrong with SACLANT or CINCHAN nor much steam behind moves to alter their responsibilities or methods of discharging them. As might be supposed, refinements are frequently suggested and none of the terms of reference is perfect. It is to the Supreme Headquarters of (the) Allied Powers in Europe (SHAPE) where the erstwhile 'Mr. Military NATO', or SACEUR, reigns that the reforming gaze is most frequently directed. This is hardly surprising when one reflects that from here operational command is exercised over something like 80 per cent of the collective Allied military effort, and that, since SACEUR has always been simultaneously appointed Commander in Chief of the United States land and air forces in Europe, he personifies the United States commitment to the Alliance. SHAPE, as we have seen in the first chapter, has very wide responsibilities, which in many ways overlap those of the Military Committee and even some of those of the political side of the house. Almost certainly the responsibilities are wider than they should be, or need be, and to the same extent they are not, and cannot be, properly discharged there, through lack of both talent (but certainly not numbers) and facilities. To the educated gaze SHAPE appears and feels and sounds like an amalgam of a Ministry of Defence and a very large field headquarters with a major communications centre superposed. It is too involved in command to deal properly with the manifold aspects of administration that it attempts, and vice versa, and it is grossly overstaffed—this being for totally irrelevant and mainly political reasons connected, bluntly, with 'keeping up with the Joneses'.

NATO should decide quickly, on the basis of the in-depth study of a command structure package such as that just recommended, what the Alliance really wants of SACEUR and his Headquarters; it can only go in the direction of some drastic slimming-down and streamlining. There are, as in the job of the Military Committee, various ways in which it could be done. One is to remove all the functions except that of actual command, while another, which goes in the diametrically opposite direction, would be to devolve the command to the Regions and let SHAPE cope with the 'admin'. Both would be full-time jobs, but unlike the present lines of control, which are very fuzzy, clear ones could be re-drawn to the advantage of SHAPE itself and all those who deal with it. Not only would very much greater efficiency result almost at once, but dramatic savings in money, men and real estate would come to hand. The overstaffing syndrome comes about at SHAPE, and in all other international headquarters, because each country insists on proportionate equivalence in numbers and ranks. This has led to a situation where any competent Inspector of Establishments could reduce SHAPE's numbers by one-third (all the way down the long chain of supporting staff) before really getting close to some arguable reductions which might save half as many again. Nearly all General officers who have served at SHAPE would agree with this, in their hearts if not in public or in their capitals.

Two simultaneous approaches should be tried if the task is to be well done and the result is to have a lean look instead of a fat one. Either devolve the command functions to the Regions, with some administration to match, and let SHAPE and Evere deal with the 'nuts and bolts' of running the machine, or what effectively would amount to the reverse. Of the two, and of course there are intermediate positions, the former is probably (though this cannot be certain until the study has been done) the better, even if SACEUR and his predecessors would be most unlikely to agree.

As part of the total organisation problem, the NATO 'image' can clearly stand a cold hard look. It needs—badly—to be enhanced if the climate of enthusiastic support which we all seek is to be created. More facts must be made more widely available, and some of the nonsensical safeguarding of material on the entirely unconvincing grounds of secrecy must be scrapped. Leading figures in the Alliance must interpret these facts and be ready to place their interpretation of them on the record and to defend it, and access must be quite freely granted to NATO exercises, briefings, study periods and demonstrations to all the family and to outsiders whether they now wish us well or not. The scope and spread of all this activity must be greatly extended to gather in our supporters and our critics alike, in schools and universities, in trades unions and above all in the media, and a great deal more money must be spent on it all. The responsibilities (rather like those for logistics) must be re-defined so that if they must remain 'national', then that must mean, and be accepted to mean, that they support and execute Alliance policy in exactly the same way as do all other national resources devoted to it. Nor will it begin to be adequate to improve the quality and quantity of those employed on NATO Public Relations, necessary though this certainly is; a far more direct and personal commitment by members of the Allied Governments is required in their own countries and outside them, all the time and not, as now, spasmodically. A good place to start would be with the communiqués after important meetings, where the drafters and Ministers themselves spend hours debating trivia instead of jointly resolving to dispense as much hard information about what they have done as possible. When the legendary man in Oshkosh Wisconsin or on the top of the Clapham omnibus really knows that NATO is not a fruit drink or an Italian football team (which is not far from what he thinks today), a promising start will have been made. It should be done at once.

The balance of conventional forces, and some special aspects of the nuclear balance, have already been dealt with at some length but mainly so as to focus attention on what can affect those balances and their relative weight. It is necessary now to look more closely at what the actual facts themselves disclose. Perhaps the first thing to note, in the light of earlier chapters, is that the situation today, and more alarmingly the forward projection of it if nothing is done, both arise precisely and directly from political will on the other side. The Soviets have never wavered in their determination to achieve the domination of the world by Communism. They have said so and continue to say so frequently and publicly. But there is no country in the world either under their domination, or still free, where Soviet Communism has been established because its people want it. They have failed, and we all share the expectation that they will continue to fail, to win the battle of ideas. Therefore their aim, if it is to be achieved, will only be achieved by naked armed power. And it is here that we see so clearly what is happening—the relentless determination to pile military might on military might until political pressure, threats or blackmail will win their game without recourse to war at all. And this is the threat—or, better, the challenge—which we must meet, or go under.

It is unnecessary to quote long lists of figures, but some facts must be quoted to give substance to this assertion. The Warsaw Pact has half a million more men under arms today than it had ten years ago, and some thirty more divisions; their total holding of tanks has risen in the same period from 47,000 to 60,000, and their factories are turning out at least 3,000 more each year. In Allied Command Europe, in broad terms, their superiority in conventional strength is not far removed from the three-to-one ratio that has been quoted as the classical requirement for successful offence. And the gigantic fleet of tank transporters, their mobile bridging equipment, their heavy self-propelled artillery and their greatly improved machinery for rapid reinforcement all add to their offensive potential in a way it is impossible to ignore.

In the air their total number of aircraft has not changed greatly; but in the vital Central Region of Europe they have significant superiority in terms of in-place tactical aircraft, and two factors have significantly increased their air power. First, modern technology has given them far greater range and hitting power; in the 1950s their Frescos could carry 500kg. about 100 miles; today, with their swing-wing Fitter Cs, their Floggers and their Fencers, they can carry up to four times the payload ten times as far. The second factor is their switch from a largely defensive configuration of these combat aircraft to an offensive one as a result of which the massive re-equipment with multi-role aircraft over the last few years now allows the Soviet commander to use almost all of his force in an offensive role if he so chooses. He can do this with the knowledge that his rear areas and homelands are now well protected by surface-to-air missiles and anti-aircraft artillery. The dramatic advance of Soviet maritime power has been the subject of a chapter on its own.

It remains to add that the Soviets' capacity to build all these advanced systems is at rates which are typically double those of the West, and in the special instances of submarines, aircraft and tanks reach a figure nearer fivefold. A good deal has also been published recently about the Soviets' emphasis on Civil Defence and, specifically, their massive investment in hardened shelters for the exercise of all elements of Government, for the protection of industry and for the survival of the population. There is no remotely comparable programme in the West. We have heard, too, of chemical warfare and note that their forces are fully equipped for the offensive use of such systems and practised in fighting in a hostile chemical warfare environment, and we have good reason to believe that their doctrine regards this element as conventional. While neither of these unique capabilities is fully measurable, nor can they ever be confidently assessed, it seems very clear that they must also be weighed in the military balance, to our disadvantage.

It is appropriate to repeat these facts simply because they are facts. They are not hypotheses, and particularly not hypotheses invented by some conspiracy of *parti-pris* Generals and Admirals to keep themselves and their jobs in business. The published literature in many countries asserts these facts and agrees upon them, and they have never been denied.

There is, in short, an unmistakable adverse trend in the balance. So what, then, is our way ahead if the adverse trend is to be arrested and reversed? What, putting it another way, must we do if we are to adhere to our vital political objectives which have never wavered, and are to enable ourselves to dispose of adequate military power to provide the defence which alone will give reality to the twin aims of deterrence and détente? First of all, can we do it? Our only potential enemies would already have won if the answer to that question were 'No'—which is why, as has been expounded at length, they pursue their search for superiority. But of course the unequivocal answer is 'Certainly we can do it—if we have the political guts—if our Governments are sufficiently determined.'

Let us look first at the more obvious elements which shine through what has been said about the military balance, and relate them to the assertion that only by studying this balance can the best way ahead be sensibly discerned. Dealing first with weapon research and development, where the Soviet Union is spending three times as much annually as the United States and twice as much as the whole of NATO, surely the remedy here is quite simple—to drive up by some quite dramatic proportion, although not necessarily a dramatic sum, the money that we spend in this essential field. Only in this way shall we maintain that superiority in quality which has perhaps been the most important counter to the inevitable numerical superiority of the other side. Next let us look very briefly at the three elements of the sea, land and air. The Supreme Allied Commanders assert, and in this have invariably had the active and positive support of the Military Committee, that they are outnumbered, and that the quality gap is closing and the facts are there which prove it. Surely it must be these facts themselves that point the way to arresting and reversing the adverse trend.

At sea we clearly need more ships and we not only need the new ships, but our existing fleets need to be brought up to date if they are to do their task in face of the increasingly hostile global deployment of the massively enlarged Soviet maritime strength. Specifically, we need a better ability to operate in the conditions imposed by modern developments; we need more point defence systems optimised against missile attack, and we need more organic air power for our Fleet Commanders, probably in the form of V/STOL aircraft of the Harrier or improved Harrier type. Certainly, ships are expensive but the other measures mentioned are relatively inexpensive, and a moment's reflection on what has already been said about the broad expanses of the North and South Atlantic, through which all supplies, reinforcements and re-supply to a European battlefield must pass, make it evident that command of the sea simply must not be surrendered. For land forces—where we do not, cannot and need not attempt to match a potential enemy man for man, tank for tank or gun for gun—we need greater firepower, and more in-place forces. We need great accuracy of all our delivery systems. We need above all, in very large numbers, relatively cheap anti-tank weapons. We need to improve our facilities for quick reinforcement, both by air and sea, and especially improved reception and onward distribution facilities in the host countries. The latter almost certainly demands the provision of adequate stockpiles of immediately ready vehicles and weapons systems and their support, so that the reinforcements can arrive by air and drive straight into action. This is expensive, but it is the only sensible answer against the numerical imbalance which cannot now be redressed. In the air we must seek to increase the numbers of our combat aircraft, and they must be high-quality and preferably multi-role. Not only these additional aircraft but our already considerable inventory of in-place and reinforcement aircraft must be of better quality to fight in a hostile electronic warfare environment. Much has been done in this field but much more remains to be done. In all these elements these are the specific pressure-points, and NATO would do well to continue the process recently begun of concentrating collectively on them, if necessary by the creation of special machinery, to work alongside the bread-and-butter business of updating the yearly plans which lead to the programme of Allied Force Goals for the five-year period ahead.

There is another balance-sheet which deserves careful consideration. This focusses on population, on wealth, on technology and on industrial capacity which can be measured; and on our democratic determination to be free to lead the lives of our choice, which cannot be measured. As regards population, that of the Allied countries is some 554 million, that of the Soviet Union 254 million and, for what it is worth (and this is at least arguable), that of the non-Soviet Warsaw Pact countries is 100 million. Can there be any reasonable shadow of doubt that a straight numerical superiority of two to one should give us a corresponding advantage? Are we mice, and the others men? Turn now to wealth where there are several commonly used criteria, but for the sake of this argument the total Gross National (or Domestic) Product will be used. That of the Allies is $2,800 billion, that of the Soviet Union is $865 billion and that of the whole Warsaw Pact is $1,135 billion. Here our advantage is more like three to one, and the question is repeated. Technology and industrial capacity are less easily quantified, but does anyone in NATO—indeed, can anyone in his senses—doubt that the West is immensely more efficient? That we produce today fewer engines of war is by choice and certainly not because of inability. So in material matters what does all this mean? Surely it must be clear that we are in the business of priorities, because the resources are there in overflowing measure. We have deliberately chosen not to use enough of them to insure our way of life, perhaps even our lives themselves.

The Alliance as a whole spends less than 5 per cent of its national income on insuring its very existence; the Soviets, by contrast, spend between 11 and 13 per cent of theirs on threatening it. There are no respectable grounds for the notion that we could not spend more—if the will were there—as the history of only this century reveals. It shows, as one would expect, that we spent what we needed to survive. What Clausewitz wrote more than a century ago on the theory of warfare is still true today: 'The possession of military or economic power is only of value if supported by political will and the readiness of the people to provide the means to defend their way of life and conception of democracy.' The test must always be to measure what we must sacrifice in order to preserve freedom against what it would mean actually to lose it, and surely to lose our freedom would be infinitely worse than the modest diversions from an easier life that are its necessary safeguard. On the lowest and most material level, where is the sense in having high standards of living and comprehensive social services if we are not able to secure and defend them? What has been said earlier about the need for a widespread and vigorous campaign to educate our public opinion in the facts of NATO life is directly relevant to the dilemma which faces democratic governments in the resource allocation bind. The necessity for leadership in such matters has been well stated by John W. Gardner:* 'An important thing to understand about any institution or social system is that it doesn't move unless it is pushed. And what is generally needed is not a mild push but a solid jolt. If the push is not administered by vigorous and purposeful leaders it will be administered eventually by an aroused citizenry or by a crisis.' The pace of international events today being what it is, we must hope that our leadership and our citizenry will be aroused well before any crisis does arise.

There is another group of problems, of a different nature, which merit consideration now because some are topical, others recurrent, and although both lots have attracted a good deal of Allied attention, there is no collective or coherent NATO policy on any of them. Let us deal first with three activities which might all be described (certainly in British handbooks) as 'aid to the Civil Power'. Here we find disaster relief, peace-keeping and dealing with hi-jackers as matters to the resolution of which NATO appears ideally placed to contribute very usefully. The Alliance disposes of people in and out of uniform with the whole range of skills and equipment needed to deal effectively with all three of these difficult issues, and has in addition an excellent worldwide network of communications, a well-oiled political machine able to take decisions quickly at the Council table, access to very extensive sources of material and money, and senior representatives of its members' national Governments resident throughout the world. There is certainly no other national or international organisation which is anything like so well equipped, but NATO has neither been asked, nor has it shown any particular enthusiasm itself, to pick up any or all of these burdens.

There are three main reasons for this, none of them very compelling and certainly not so discouraging as to make another determined effort not worthwhile. The first and most important, which influences the other two, is politics at both the national and the international levels. NATO is not a world organisation such as the United Nations Organisation, and the

* In *The Recovery of Confidence*, New York: W. W. Norton, 1970, p. 93.

Treaty which delineates its objectives very clearly could also be held to delineate by omission what it is not in business to do. There is an evident collective and individual reluctance among its members to dip their toes in what, in these affairs, can well be very hot water. In peace-keeping, for example, the forces of certain members would be not only unwelcome but actually unacceptable in, say, Cyprus or Southern Africa or North Africa. There is also an understandable fear in the Alliance of becoming involved in an activity the costs of which are open-ended, certainly unpredictable and potentially high, against a general background of inadequate resources being made available for the proper discharge of accepted Alliance responsibilities. Thirdly, the actual use of the armed forces and their facilities and their equipment is, in peacetime, not under NATO control but entirely a matter for their parent-governments. All these difficulties are real but do not seem on careful analysis to be insuperable, most certainly not in all such matters, if there were a collective determination to overcome them. There can be no doubt that the means are available, the political problems could nearly always be solved, and much good would accrue to the standing of NATO in the eyes of the world, and to those actually afflicted, were the Council to be encouraged not to rehearse the difficulties but to make firm proposals for their resolution. Imagination, courage and drive would be needed to venture into such new fields but there is no shortage of these qualities in either the capitals or the Headquarters of the Alliance, and much benefit would undoubtedly follow success.

A second problem in this group of those of a different nature is that posed by Euro-Communism, which has been of considerable concern to the Council, to the Military Committee and to the millions of people they represent, ever since it reared its head in earnest in the middle 1970s. The clearest evidence of this is probably the fact that for the last three or four years virtually no Allied leader has given a press conference or interview on any NATO topic without being asked for his views on the effect which Euro-Communism could have, or already has, on the Alliance and particularly on its political and military cohesion. One of the main difficulties in answering this and similar questions is the lack of a commonly agreed definition or description of the subject, even among its leading Western European proponents such as Signor Berlinguer, Señor Carrillo and M. Marchais. The British Foreign Secretary was reported in November 1977 as having referred in derogatory terms to 'trendy slogans, such as Euro-Communism [which is] a dangerous term conferring respectability on an ill-defined, disparate, and as yet un-identifiable phenomenon', and it would be hard for anyone sharing that view (as many do) to answer the interview question posed above. It is necessary to remember that NATO is not, and never has been, an anti-Communist alliance, although there are none so simple as not to recognise that in its history hitherto the Soviet Communists have been the only potential aggressors. Thus the 'phenomenon' of Euro-Communism is bound to raise very grave questions indeed if any Allied Government were to be dominated by those professing it, or if such people formed part of any of our Governments.

Two dominant questions would immediately arise if such a situation came to pass. Would Governments dominated by or partly composed of Communists continue to support the Allied military effort and could Allied security (in the Intelligence field) remain intact? Put another way, would Communists in the Government of any NATO country be, in reality, a 'Trojan horse' intended to infiltrate and undermine the democratic Alliance? The answers must be that nobody knows, if for no other reason than that it has not yet happened. NATO has, however, 'managed' successfully the occasions when Communist Ministers formed part of the Governments of Iceland and Portugal, and they would undoubtedly do the same if they were in the future to form part of, say, an Italian or French Administration. Their actual reaction, however, would have to be pragmatic, and it would depend largely on the influence that such Ministers would be deemed to have on their national policies, especially in Foreign Affairs, Defence and Finance. There are those, including Dr. Kissinger, who take a more robust view, on the general lines of 'a Communist is a Communist whatever you put before or after his name and the only safe procedure is to regard him as a potential opponent'. The former approach—to deal with each manifestation on a case-by-case basis—would seem more elegant, and more likely to succeed.

To complete this brief look at what may well become an extremely awkward puzzle, reference must be made to the view, taken by a number of people, that 'the enemy within' is actually more dangerous than the potential enemy without, and has indeed already caused a significant reduction in NATO's military posture. There is no evidence—and it has been diligently sought—for such a view. Our armed forces have been neither diverted from the Allied order of battle nor subverted from their commitment to it, and there is no present reason to suppose that either of these disasters impends. Also, neither the political nor the military leaders of NATO are other than keenly aware that here too, as SACEUR's official motto has it, 'vigilance is the price of liberty'.

This passage about some of NATO's problems which are out of the mainstream of Alliance business, and what has been said about nearly all the other problems in earlier chapters, have been based upon the conventional wisdom. They have included what must be deemed to be the dominant financial, political and consequential military facts of NATO life today and tomorrow. None of them demands a re-appraisal of our aim, although their combined and collective weight, taken together, must demand positive and early remedial action if the balance, above all in conventional forces, is to be restored to that equilibrium where deterrence is manifest. This is to demand a return to first principles and not a new policy.

There is however another dimension in which there are quite strong arguments for, if not a re-appraisal, then certainly some careful thought, about NATO policy. What immediately follows is not conventional wisdom but a personal view which the author is happy to share with many important political as well as military figures in the Alliance. First, there is the clear lack of a coherent NATO policy which relates the problems of the Central Region to the quite different ones of the Northern and Southern Regions and the Atlantic. Secondly, there is the manifest threat to the wellbeing of the Allies, collectively and separately, from events outside the arbitrary boundaries of the NATO area.

Let us consider the latter first. The boundaries of the NATO area are geopolitical, if that means that they are delineated geographically but chosen for political reasons. They are most certainly not chosen for military reasons. Also, they were laid down in Alliance terms a long time ago because they are to be found in the Treaty itself, and in protocols to the Treaty executed at the time of Greek and Turkish accession, at German accession and with the independence (from France) of Algeria. Effectively the boundaries amount to the territories of the signatories and the sea- and air-space around them but—and it is a big and important 'but'—the southern limit of the two latter was declared to be the Tropic of Cancer. What has already been said about the dramatic growth of Soviet maritime power is given (if it were needed) even greater importance by this arbitrary line on NATO maps and the fact that there are no such lines on Soviet maps. The reasons for selecting the Tropic of Cancer in 1949 are obscure, and in fact they no longer matter. At the time, the Soviet Navy was a small coast-defence force which did not and could not keep the blue water. Indeed it is doubtful whether any of its vessels could have reached the Tropic of Cancer, and highly unlikely that if they had done so they could have achieved anything military. But today, with their forward operating bases in East and West Africa, they straddle the vital sea lines of communication through which much more than half of Western Europe's food, energy and the raw materials for industry must come, and indeed upon which North America too is now dependent.

The other boundaries remain arbitrary although the political considerations which led to their geographical limits are now vastly different from what they were, and it is this which permits and provokes consideration of another dimension. NATO was not, in the first years of its life, faced with events outside its boundaries which could have the most profound effect on the Allies separately and collectively. Perhaps this began to change with the Cuban crisis in 1962, and it certainly continued to change with successive Middle East wars, with the war and threats of war in South-East Asia, with the energy crisis, with Angola and with events in Southern Africa. The change has been difficult to deal with in NATO. Machinery at the political level certainly exists for the discussion of happenings of all sorts all round the globe, but it is neither necessary nor customary for the Council to reach a collective view on them, much less to develop policies to cope with their effect on member-states. Still less is done, or is allowed to be done, by the NATO military authorities, although if ever there was a desperate need for joint and early and resolute planning, it must be in the protection of these literally vital supply lines.

Should NATO look outside these unchanged boundaries? The answer must be 'Yes'. Is it right that one Ally, deeply involved in the support of a war outside NATO, should ask for and be refused passive facilities by her NATO Allies? Surely the answer to this must be 'No'—certainly if the ill-feeling engendered by such a situation during the Yom Kippur war of 1973 between the United States and several European partners is to be avoided in future. Was it right that the Allies should formulate no collective policy over such dire crises as those in Berlin (on four occasions), Hungary and Czechoslovakia, until after the event? Surely the answer here too must be 'No'.

Coming much closer to the present time, in 1975 NATO watched, passively, the first projection of Soviet military power and political influence outside the Euro-Asian land mass in the rape, by proxy Cuban forces, of Angola. This was, it may be added parenthetically, an excellent example of options opening when the military capability and political will are there—or closing very fast if they are lacking.

There was, and continues to be, a great deal of talk about all this both in capitals and at Evere and heads are nodded wisely, but nothing practical has been done which might allow the Alliance to cope collectively and coherently with such crises outside our boundaries in future. The Council discusses Southern Africa, and foresees the dire events which may quite well occur there, but there is, to be blunt, no NATO policy which might apply outside the NATO area. Perhaps this is legalistically right; perhaps it is technically too difficult to change this potentially disastrous limitation on Allied room for manoeuvre; but there can surely be few who would think it is wise.

To come from the particular to the general, with the imperatives of our supply lines and the disastrous consequences which would at once follow their interruption, compounded by the arbitrary and self-imposed limit of our southern maritime boundary which positively prevents any collective defence below the Tropic of Cancer, and compounded further by today's Soviet maritime power, the finger of fate points inexorably to South Africa. Any experienced NATO hand knows that the Allies are united in their detestation of the South African Government, and so does everybody else who has not been living on Mars, but this will not make the highly uncomfortable facts of life just rehearsed go away. South Africa produces three-quarters of the West's gold, she has three-quarters of the world's known reserves of chrome and is second only to the Soviet Union in its production, she has a similar share in industrial diamonds, and is second only to the United States in the production of uranium which, even if not needed for nuclear weapons, must surely in future be needed for nuclear power. These too are hard facts which bite deep into the sinews of NATO's defensive and economic security, and are no more likely to go away than are the others. All these undeniable facts, however unwelcome they may be to governments dedicated to the abolition of apartheid, make it mandatory for the Alliance to devise adequate defence of the Cape route, and thus a deterrent to attempts to deny it to both Western Europe and North America. No serious effort has yet been made to do so, and the facts insist that it must be done, and done before this palpable weakness becomes too attractive an option for a would-be aggressor to resist.

To return to the first point of the other dimension with which this passage began, it is rather similar to the second point in its nature though not in terms of scope or geography. NATO has always looked inwards, and for historical reasons which go back for centuries, it has been hypnotised by the Central Region. It is there that, as has already been somewhat poetically said, a million men on each side, armed and equipped in all respects for Armageddon, stand eyeball to eyeball. There lies the route to the heartland of NATO, to the Channel ports, to our great industries and energy plants, to Germany, to France and even to the Atlantic and the Mediterranean. The reasons for this hypnosis are legion and compelling but it is at least questionable whether they are any longer wise counsellors.

Certainly these immensely important political, military, material and human assets must be properly protected. Certainly no soft options must be offered to a would-be aggressor especially if it were a *fait accompli* achieved perhaps by surprise attack (which, as we have seen, has been a favourite subject for much romantic and not very well-informed speculation), but it is highly important to question closely whether there are too many NATO eggs in this Central Region basket at a time when eggs are scarce.

What is certainly true is that it is very hard work indeed to persuade even the Council and the Military Committee to give any serious weight, much less due weight, to the Flanks or to the lifeline that leads to the whole of Europe from our only source of reinforcements and, in times of peace but still more in times of tension or war, our only sources of energy, food and raw materials. Does history not show that an aggressor will always seek chinks in the defender's armour, and are the Soviets not past-masters of the probe and the exploitation of any weakness it may disclose? Is any competent authority content with the situation in Greece, Turkey and the Mediterranean, or in Finnmark? It is hard not to be concerned lest the weaknesses present there, and in the Atlantic, are almost literally asking for trouble.

Plainly NATO today is neither ready nor willing, and neither organised nor structured, to deal satisfactorily with these two (and they are not exclusive) examples of problems in what has, perhaps not very aptly, been called another dimension. It can be argued that it is not intended that the Alliance should do so, and the Treaty can be prayed in aid to prove it. In the same way, NATO has never pretended to be in any sense a world policeman and has not sought a role on the political stage outside the Treaty area. It is, nevertheless, very much in the separate and collective interests of all the Allies that coherent and joint policies should emerge about any matter which could affect their societies, be it in the domain of security or commerce or industry. NATO has, after all, and with excellent reason, come to be highly regarded as the corporate guardian of the ideals of democracy by many non-member-states which share them.

Is this a practical proposition? In principle the answer must surely be 'Yes', but in practice many fairly high and awkward hurdles would have to be negotiated before even a start could be made. The approach most likely to lead most quickly to useful progress would be to focus on making better use of the immense reservoir of talent which already exists both at Evere and in the member-capitals, and to let self-interest point the way to the wider scene. NATO and its individual members are, after all, formally pledged to 'consult together whenever, in the opinion of any of them, the territorial integrity, political independence or security of any of the parties is threatened'. Moreover it is expressly stated in the Ottawa Declaration that '. . . they [the Allies] are firmly resolved to keep each other fully informed and to strengthen the practice of frank and timely consultations by all means which may be appropriate on matters relating to their common interests as members of the Alliance, bearing in mind that these interests can be affected by events in other areas of the world.' No further licence or encouragement to grasp this awkward nettle is therefore necessary. It can hardly be denied that the crises already mentioned qualified unreservedly for 'frank and timely consultations' or that they could (and did) 'relate to their common interests as members of the Alliance'. So it is certainly a respectable, even if possibly controversial, view that the establishment of stability in, for example, the Middle East and Southern Africa qualify equally unreservedly.

Here then is some unconventional wisdom on a field of endeavour which NATO is lavishly equipped to enter and where common prudence demands that much more should be done. It is long past time to make the inward-looking Allies twitch aside their lace curtains and peer carefully and thoroughly out of the window at what the neighbours are doing, so that the way ahead may be more usefully discerned.

In this rather lengthy survey of problems of widely differing importance and character and suggestions for their treatment, it is not intended to imply that any of them is new, or that all of them are not at some time on the agenda in capitals and at Evere. There is, as must be clear, an immense mass of complex and interlocking problems each of which bears directly on the basic objectives, the policy and the strategy of the North Atlantic Treaty Organisation. It must be equally clear that to resolve them all, and to keep them under orderly control and to face and overcome new ones will all take time. Their rehearsal may be concluded with a reminder that when, during the Second World War, someone told General de Gaulle that what he was proposing would take fifty years to accomplish, the great man replied: 'All the more reason for starting now.'

ENVOI

It is demanded of this sort of work that, to convince, it should not be a collection of multitudinous impressions but should depict the sharp edges. NATO, by its nature and its history, has no shortage of sharp edges and a fair sample of them has been selected for examination. But because the Alliance is such a vast enterprise, some impressions must go with the sharp edges if an adequate 'feel' for the whole problem is to be conveyed, and so these too have been included.

NATO is all about the collective security, not only in the military field, of fifteen democracies with closely similar hopes and fears. The Alliance will continue to succeed, or it will begin to fail, in reaching this dominant objective precisely in proportion to the political will that its member-governments display separately and collectively in its support. This political will itself depends upon a clear understanding of the facts of NATO life, and a sober evaluation of them, by public opinion as well as by Parliaments. This book is intended to encourage the process by shedding light on the facts which really matter in judging NATO, and by offering a personal evaluation of most of them. Some of this will certainly not be welcome in various quarters, but that is the best of reasons for setting it all out, in the hope of driving home the indelible lesson that soft options will nearly always lead to disaster.

A character in a play by Montherlant said: 'If you are telling me all that to put my mind at rest, I should tell you that men of my calling were not intended to have our minds at rest.' It is to be hoped that this work will have been read in that spirit. *Nunc dimittis.*

APPENDIX A

ARTICLE 51 OF
THE CHARTER OF THE UNITED NATIONS
(*24 October 1945*)

Nothing in the present Charter shall impair the inherent right of individual or collective self-defence if an armed attack occurs against a Member of the United Nations, until the Security Council has taken measures necessary to maintain international peace and security. Measures taken by Members in the exercise of this right of self-defence shall be immediately reported to the Security Council and shall not in any way affect the authority and responsibility of the Security Council under the present Charter to take at any time such action as it deems necessary in order to maintain or restore international peace and security.

THE NORTH ATLANTIC TREATY

(Washington D.C., 4 April 1949)

The Parties to this Treaty reaffirm their faith in the purposes and principles of the Charter of the United Nations and their desire to live in peace with all peoples and all governments.

They are determined to safeguard the freedom, common heritage and civilisation of their peoples, founded on the principles of democracy, individual liberty and the rule of law.

They seek to promote stability and well-being in the North Atlantic area.

They are resolved to unite their efforts for collective defence and for the preservation of peace and security.

They therefore agree to this North Atlantic Treaty:

ARTICLE 1
The Parties undertake, as set forth in the Charter of the United Nations, to settle any international dispute in which they may be involved by peaceful means in such a manner that international peace and security and justice are not endangered, and to refrain in their international relations from the threat or use of force in any manner inconsistent with the purposes of the United Nations.

ARTICLE 2
The Parties will contribute toward the further development of peaceful and friendly international relations by strengthening their free institutions, by bringing about a better understanding of the principles upon which these institutions are founded, and by promoting conditions of stability and well-being. They will seek to eliminate conflict in their international economic policies and will encourage economic collaboration between any or all of them.

ARTICLE 3
In order more effectively to achieve the objectives of this Treaty, the Parties, separately and jointly, by means of continuous and effective self-help and mutual aid, will maintain and develop their individual and collective capacity to resist armed attack.

ARTICLE 4

The Parties will consult together whenever, in the opinion of any of them, the territorial integrity, political independence or security of any of the Parties is threatened.

ARTICLE 5

The Parties agree that an armed attack against one or more of them in Europe or North America shall be considered an attack against them all and consequently they agree that, if such an armed attack occurs, each of them, in exercise of the right of individual or collective self-defence recognised by Article 51 of the Charter of the United Nations, will assist the Party or Parties so attacked by taking forthwith, individually and in concert with the other Parties, such action as it deems necessary, including the use of armed force, to restore and maintain the security of the North Atlantic area.

Any such armed attack and all measures taken as a result thereof shall immediately be reported to the Security Council. Such measures shall be terminated when the Security Council has taken the measures necessary to restore and maintain international peace and security.

ARTICLE 6

For the purpose of Article 5 an armed attack on one or more of the Parties is deemed to include an armed attack on the territory of any of the Parties in Europe or North America, on the Algerian Departments of France, on the occupation forces of any Party in Europe, on the islands under the jurisdiction of any Party in the North Atlantic area north of the Tropic of Cancer or on the vessels or aircraft in this area of any of the Parties.

ARTICLE 7

This Treaty does not affect, and shall not be interpreted as affecting, in any way the rights and obligations under the Charter of the Parties which are members of the United Nations, or the primary responsibility of the Security Council for the maintenance of international peace and security.

ARTICLE 8

Each Party declares that none of the international engagements now in force between it and any other of the Parties or any third State is in conflict with the provisions of this Treaty, and undertakes not to enter into any international engagement in conflict with this Treaty.

ARTICLE 9

The Parties hereby establish a Council, on which each of them shall
be represented, to consider matters concerning the implementation
of this Treaty. The Council shall be so organised as to be able to
meet promptly at any time. The Council shall set up such subsidiary
bodies as may be necessary; in particular it shall establish immediately a defence committee which shall recommend measures for the
implementation of Articles 3 and 5.

ARTICLE 10

The Parties may, by unanimous agreement, invite any other
European State in a position to further the principles of this Treaty
and to contribute to the security of the North Atlantic area to accede
to this Treaty. Any State so invited may become a Party to the
Treaty by depositing its instrument of accession with the Government of the United States of America. The Government of the
United States of America will inform each of the Parties of the
deposit of each such instrument of accession.

ARTICLE 11

This Treaty shall be ratified and its provisions carried out by the
Parties in accordance with their respective constitutional processes.
The instruments of ratification shall be deposited as soon as possible
with the Government of the United States of America, which will
notify all the other signatories of each deposit. The Treaty shall
enter into force between the States which have ratified it as soon as
the ratifications of the majority of the signatories, including the
ratifications of Belgium, Canada, France, Luxembourg, the
Netherlands, the United Kingdom and the United States, have
been deposited and shall come into effect with respect to other
States on the date of the deposit of their ratifications.

ARTICLE 12

After the Treaty has been in force for ten years, or at any time
thereafter, the Parties shall, if any of them so requests, consult
together for the purpose of reviewing the Treaty, having regard for
the factors then affecting peace and security in the North Atlantic
area, including the development of universal as well as regional
arrangements under the Charter of the United Nations for the
maintenance of international peace and security.

ARTICLE 13

After the Treaty has been in force for twenty years, any Party may cease to be a Party one year after its notice of denunciation has been given to the Government of the United States of America, which will inform the Governments of the other Parties of the deposit of each notice of denunciation.

ARTICLE 14

This Treaty, of which the English and French texts are equally authentic, shall be deposited in the archives of the Government of the United States of America. Duly certified copies will be transmitted by that Government to the Governments of other signatories.

The definition of the territories to which Article 5 applies was revised by Article 11 of the Protocol to the North Atlantic Treaty on the accession of Greece and Turkey.

APPENDIX C

DECLARATION ON ATLANTIC RELATIONS

This declaration was approved and published by the North Atlantic Council in Ottawa on 19 June 1974 and signed by Heads of NATO Governments in Brussels on 26 June 1974.

1. The members of the North Atlantic Alliance declare that the Treaty signed 25 years ago to protect their freedom and independence has confirmed their common destiny. Under the shield of the Treaty, the Allies have maintained their security, permitting them to preserve the values which are the heritage of their civilisation and enabling Western Europe to rebuild from its ruins and lay the foundations of its unity.

2. The members of the Alliance reaffirm their conviction that the North Atlantic Treaty provides the indispensable basis for their security, thus making possible the pursuit of détente. They welcome the progress that has been achieved on the road towards détente and harmony among nations, and the fact that a Conference of 35 countries of Europe and North America is now seeking to lay down guidelines designed to increase security and co-operation in Europe. They believe that until circumstances permit the introduction of general, complete and controlled disarmament, which alone could provide genuine security for all, the ties uniting them must be maintained. The Allies share a common desire to reduce the burden of arms expenditure on their peoples. But States that wish to preserve peace have never achieved this aim by neglecting their own security.

3. The members of the Alliance reaffirm that their common defence is one and indivisible. An attack on one or more of them in the area of application of the Treaty shall be considered an attack against them all. The common aim is to prevent any attempt by a foreign power to threaten the independence or integrity of a member of the Alliance. Such an attempt would not only put in jeopardy the security of all members of the Alliance but also threaten the foundations of world peace.

4. At the same time they realize that the circumstances affecting their common defence have profoundly changed in the last ten years: the strategic relationship between the United States and the

164

Soviet Union has reached a point of near equilibrium. Consequently, although all the countries of the Alliance remain vulnerable to attack, the nature of the danger to which they are exposed has changed. The Alliance's problems in the defence of Europe have thus assumed a different and more distinct character.

5. However, the essential elements in the situation which gave rise to the Treaty have not changed. While the commitment of all the Allies to the common defence reduces the risk of external aggression, the contribution to the security of the entire Alliance provided by the nuclear forces of the United States based in the United States as well as in Europe and by the presence of North American forces in Europe remains indispensable.

6. Nevertheless, the Alliance must pay careful attention to the dangers to which it is exposed in the European region, and must adopt all measures necessary to avert them. The European members who provide three-quarters of the conventional strength of the Alliance in Europe, and two of whom possess nuclear forces capable of playing a deterrent role of their own, contributing to the overall strengthening of the deterrence of the Alliance, undertake to make the necessary contribution to maintain the common defence at a level capable of deterring and if necessary repelling all actions directed against the independence and territorial integrity of the members of the Alliance.

7. The United States, for its part, reaffirms its determination not to accept any situation which would expose its Allies to external political or military pressure likely to deprive them of their freedom, and states its resolve, together with its Allies, to maintain forces in Europe at the level required to sustain the credibility of the strategy of deterrence and to maintain the capacity to defend the North Atlantic area should deterrence fail.

8. In this connection the member states of the Alliance affirm that as the ultimate purpose of any defence policy is to deny to a potential adversary the objectives he seeks to attain through an armed conflict, all necessary forces would be used for this purpose. Therefore, while reaffirming that a major aim of their policies is to seek agreements that will reduce the risk of war, they also state that such agreements will not limit their freedom to use all forces at their disposal for the common defence in case of attack. Indeed, they are convinced that their determination to do so continues to be the best assurance that war in all its forms will be prevented.

9. All members of the Alliance agree that the continued presence of Canadian and substantial US forces in Europe plays an irreplaceable role in the defence of North America as well as of Europe.

Similarly the substantial forces of the European Allies serve to defend Europe and North America as well. It is also recognised that the further progress towards unity, which the member states of the European Community are determined to make, should in due course have a beneficial effect on the contribution to the common defence of the Alliance of those of them who belong to it. Moreover, the contributions made by members of the Alliance to the preservation of international security and world peace are recognised to be of great importance.

10. The members of the Alliance consider that the will to combine their efforts to ensure their common defence obliges them to maintain and improve the efficiency of their forces and that each should undertake, according to the role that it has assumed in the structure of the Alliance, its proper share of the burden of maintaining the security of all. Conversely, they take the view that in the course of current or future negotiations nothing must be accepted which could diminish this security.

11. The Allies are convinced that the fulfilment of their common aims requires the maintenance of close consultation, co-operation and mutual trust, thus fostering the conditions necessary for defence and favourable for détente, which are complementary. In the spirit of the friendship, equality and solidarity which characterise their relationship, they are firmly resolved to keep each other fully informed and to strengthen the practice of frank and timely consultations by all means which may be appropriate on matters relating to their common interests as members of the Alliance, bearing in mind that these interests can be affected by events in other areas of the world. They wish also to ensure that their essential security relationship is supported by harmonious political and economic relations. In particular they will work to remove sources of conflict between their economic policies and to encourage economic co-operation with one another.

12. They recall that they have proclaimed their dedication to the principles of democracy, respect for human rights, justice and social progress, which are the fruits of their shared spiritual heritage and they declare their intention to develop and deepen the application of these principles in their countries. Since these principles, by their very nature, forbid any recourse to methods incompatible with the promotion of world peace, they reaffirm that the efforts which they make to preserve their independence, to maintain their security and to improve the living standards of their peoples exclude all forms of aggression against anyone, are not directed against any other country, and are designed to bring about the general improvement

of international relations. In Europe, their objective continues to be the pursuit of understanding and co-operation with every European country. In the world at large, each Allied country recognises the duty to help the developing countries. It is in the interest of all that every country benefit from technical and economic progress in an open and equitable world system.

13. They recognise that the cohesion of the Alliance has found expression not only in co-operation among their governments, but also in the free exchange of views among the elected representatives of the peoples of the Alliance. Accordingly, they declare their support for the strengthening of links among Parliamentarians.

14. The members of the Alliance rededicate themselves to the aims and ideals of the North Atlantic Treaty during this year of the twenty-fifth Anniversary of its signature. The member nations look to the future, confident that the vitality and creativity of their peoples are commensurate with the challenges which confront them. They declare their conviction that the North Atlantic Alliance continues to serve as an essential element in the lasting structure of peace they are determined to build.

NOTES ON SOURCES

I am indebted to the following sources which were used in the preparation of this book. All statistics, however expressed, come without exception from published and unclassified sources.

Daily and weekly press, the United Kingdom, the U.S.A. and Western Europe.

NATO Review. Articles by Lord Brimelow, Wiegand Pabsch (Détente), Hill-Norton (Crisis Management), *et al.*

NATO Facts and Figures (NATO Information Service).

The Military Balance (annual publication), International Institute for Strategic Studies, London.

The Author's unclassified lectures at the Royal United Services Institution, London; the Royal Institute of International Affairs, London; and at seminars in Cambridge (England), Brussels, Paris, Munich, etc.

Lectures at the Royal United Services Institute, London, by Lord Home of the Hirsel, SACEUR, *et al.*

Anglo-German dialogue ('Some Problems of Détente'), Brussels, November 1976.

NATO basic documents, including communiqués. Other NATO documents, including: 'Report on Non-military Co-operation in NATO' (report of Committee of Three), 1956; 'Future Tasks of the Alliance' (the 'Harmel Report'), 1967; 'Political Consulation', n.d.

Western European Union Committee, Report no. 757 ('Communications and Crisis Management in the Alliance'), 4 Nov. 1977.

U.S. Congressional Record.

Nunn, Senator Sam, unclassified report to NATO Joint Committee.

Robinson, N.T.N. (Middleburg, Va., U.S.A.), 'The Ground Launched Cruise Missile and NATO Defense' (memorandum), June 1977.

Godson, Joseph, *Transatlantic Crisis*, International Herald Tribune, 1974.

Burgess, W. Randolph, and James R. Huntley, *Europe and America*, New York: Walker Publ. Co., 1970.

INDEX

Defence College (NATO), Rome, 88
Defence Committee, 5, 7, 10
Defence Planning Committee, 5–6,
12, 84, 88, 89, 105, 106, 113, 137,
138, 139
Denmark, 3, 53–5
Détente, 9, 13, 18, 19, 97, 130ff.

Eisenhower, General, 10
Elizabeth II, Queen, 11
Escalation, On (book by Herman
Kahn), 48
Euro-Communism, 149–50
Eurogroup, 120
European Defence Improvement
Programme (EDIP), 14
European Economic Community
(EEC), 79, 91
Evere (NATO headquarters, near
Brussels), 11, 53
Exercises (NATO), 106, 123–5

Financial aspects of NATO, 81, 82,
90, 113–4, 147
Financial and Economic Committee,
5
Finnmark (Norway), 12, 54, 155
Flexible response, 25, 43–4, 94ff.,
103
France: 3, 7, 56, 57, 66, 73–5, 86,
152, 154; possession of nuclear
deterrent, 24, 74; military withdrawal from NATO and consequences, 4, 6, 7, 8, 11, 73, 100;
Military Mission to Military
Committee, 88–9; defence
industry, 120–1

Gardner, John W., 148
Gaulle, General de, 157
German Democratic Republic, 17,
100; navy, 30
Germany, Federal Republic of, 3,
10, 24, 35, 53, 71–2, 113, 120, 152,
154
Gorschkov, Admiral Sergei, 19,
62–3

Greece, 3, 57, 72–3, 152, 154;
withdrawal from integrated military structure, 6

Harmel Report, 9, 133
Heusinger, General, 8
Hiroshima, 43, 47
Home, Lord, of the Hirsel, 24
Hungary, 17, 40, 100, 103, 153
Huxley, Sir Andrew, ix, 18

Iceland, 3, 7, 88, 150
Independent European Programme
Group, 121
Indian Ocean, 67
Infrastructure of NATO, 114–5
Intelligence, 40, 64, 105
International Military Staff, 87–8
Iron Curtain, 2, 3, 17
Ismay, General Lord, 1, 10
Italy, 3, 57, 72

Kahn, Herman, 48, 52, 99
Khrushchev, N., 102, 131
Kissinger, Dr H., 150
Kølsas, 57
Kutusov, General, 122

Lasers, 32, 48
Leber, Georg (W. German Defence
Minister), 84
Liddell Hart, Capt. B., 29–30, 31
Lipson, Prof., 99, 103
Lisbon, meeting of NATO Council
at (1962), 5, 10
Logistics, 34, 35, 81, 125–7

McNamara, Robert, 104
Mahan, Captain, 59, 62
Malaya, 17, 29
Marchais, Georges, 150
Marshall, General, and Marshall
Plan, 3
Mediterranean, 13, 57, 67, 154, 155
Military Agency for Standardi-
sation, 88

Military Balance, The (annual publication, International Institute for Strategic Studies), 28
Military Committee, 7, 8, 9, 11, 12, 81, 82, 85, 86, 87, 88, 89, 105, 106, 111, 115, 123, 124, 137, 138, 139, 140, 145, 149, 155
Military Representatives, 7, 105
Missiles, nuclear, 44–7, 49, 50, 51, 64, 65
Montgomery, Field Marshal, 3
Mutual and Balanced Force Reductions (MBFR), 13, 32, 87, 133–4, 135

Naples (headquarters, NATO Southern Region), 56
Naval on-call force (Mediterranean), 13
Neutron bomb, 48, 135
North Atlantic Council, *see* Council
North Atlantic Treaty, *see* Treaty
North Sea, 54
Norway, 3, 53–4, 55
Nuclear Defence Affairs Committee, 6, 12, 84
Nuclear Planning Group, 12, 84

Okean 75 exercise, 124
Ottawa Declaration, 14, 85, 92, 133, 156; (text) 164–7

Poland, 17, 40, 100; navy, 30
Portugal, 3, 150; role in Alliance, 78
Public Relations and the 'image' of NATO, 81, 112–13, 142

Reinforcements, 34ff.
Reykjavik Signal, 13, 133
Romania, 18
Royal Air Force, 75–6
Royal Navy, 75

Schlesinger, Dr, 28
Schleswig-Holstein, 55

Secretary General of NATO, 6, 87, 91, 99, 139
SHAPE, *see* Supreme Headquarters
Situation Centre, 104–5
Smart, Ian, 52
Southern Africa, 135, 149, 152, 153, 154, 156
Soviet Union: 2, 17; world strategy, 9, 143; threat to Western Europe, 24, 103; maritime power, 60ff., 153; nuclear missile capability, 44–7, 49ff.; troop rotations, 36
Sovmedron, 67
Spain, 79–80, 123
Staerke, André de, 11
Stalin, Joseph, 3
Standardisation, 81, 115ff.; *see also* Military Agency
Standing Group (NATO), 7, 8, 86
Submarines, 30, 45, 64, 65–6, 135, 144
'Support', 33–4
Supreme Allied Commander Atlantic (SACLANT), 10, 59, 76, 78, 87, 88, 140
Supreme Allied Commander Europe (SACEUR), 9, 10, 11, 73, 76, 78, 86, 87, 88, 99, 124, 139, 140, 141, 151
Supreme Headquarters of the Allied Powers in Europe (SHAPE), 140–1
Surprise attack, 31, 107, 108

Tanks, 26, 30, 144
'Three Wise Men', 9
Training, 38
Treaty, North Atlantic, 1, 3, 16–17, 85, 93; signed in Washington, 21, 22; its dual nature, 3
'Trip-wire' and massive nuclear retaliation, 24, 44, 94ff.
Truman, President, and Truman doctrine, 2–3
Turkey, 3, 57, 72–3, 152, 154